Volume VII

No. 77

March, 1970

Second edition

TOWARD THERAPEUTIC CARE

**A GUIDE FOR THOSE WHO WORK
WITH THE MENTALLY ILL**

**FORMULATED BY
THE COMMITTEE ON THERAPEUTIC CARE**

GROUP FOR THE ADVANCEMENT OF PSYCHIATRY

Standard Book Number 87318-106-9

Library of Congress Catalog Card Number 62-2872

Printed in the United States of America

Second edition, March, 1970

TABLE OF CONTENTS

PART THREE—GUIDE FOR USING CLINICAL
CASE STUDIES

The page numbers in this Table of Contents are taken from the folios that appear at the bottom of the pages of this book. The numbers at the top of the pages identify them in their appropriate sequence in the Volume 7 Series of publications of the Group for the Advancement of Psychiatry, of which this guide is a part.

PREFACE

Since its publication eight years ago* TOWARD THERAPEU-
TIC CARE has enjoyed wide acceptance by both professionals
and non-professionals involved in the care and treatment of
the emotionally and mentally ill. Comments and suggestions
have been received from Alaska to New Zealand, and from
all the continents. They have indicated an increasing use of
the manual in areas outside pure nursing—as we had hoped.
This extension into the broader field of mental health at
levels below the sophisticated-professional underscored the
need for help in the use of TOWARD THERAPEUTIC CARE for
teaching and supervisory purposes. It became apparent that
technical assistance might be of considerable benefit to those
who were using the manual and to others who might need it.
The great expansion of resources for the treatment of the
mentally ill as exemplified by the growth of mental health
centers and a hierarchy of pre- and post-hospital modalities
would undoubtedly increase the numbers and types of less
professionalized persons involved in mental health programs.
These would undoubtedly benefit considerably from an approach as presented by TOWARD THERAPEUTIC CARE and
would require training and instruction in large numbers by
less sophisticated and non-professional teachers and supervisors.

This second edition of the manual has three components:
(1) The revision of the original text. All comments indicated
that this was substantially sound, and most revisions have
been in the direction of greater clarity of expression, the fundamental principles remaining unchanged. (2) The updating
of the Selective Reference List by the addition of over 40

---

* See Foreword to original edition on page vii.

additional titles. (3) The addition of a guide for using the clinical case studies in the light of the text, a guide which should be useful to anyone involved in the training and supervision of those who work with the emotionally and mentally ill in professional and non-professional capacities. To accomplish this, a third part was written titled *Guide for Using Clinical Case Studies.*

This new part was written entirely by two of the consultants who worked with the Committee on the writing of the original edition: Barbara B. Buchanan, R.N., and Helen K. Sainato, R.N. Both Mrs. Buchanan and Mrs. Sainato have been using TOWARD THERAPEUTIC CARE over the last eight years in the teaching and supervision of all classes of persons working in the field of mental health. Part Three is the result of their long and extensive experience in using the original, and it is hoped that this will further amplify its usefulness in all the many areas where TOWARD THERAPEUTIC CARE may have application in the "therapeutic use of the self" for the better care of the emotionally and mentally ill wherever and by whom they are treated.

*Committee on Therapeutic Care**
Group for the Advancement of Psychiatry

---

* The Committee on Therapeutic Care was known as the Committee on Psychiatric Nursing when it formulated the original report that was published in October, 1961, under the title TOWARD THERAPEUTIC CARE. At that time Dr. Benjamin Simon was chairman of the Committee on Psychiatric Nursing. Dr. Simon also served as chairman of the present Committee on Therapeutic Care during the period when this second edition of TOWARD THERAPEUTIC CARE was completed.

At the time the Committee on Psychiatric Nursing formulated the original report, it also included the following members: Marvin L. Adland, Ian L. W. Clancey, Thomas E. Curtis, Robert W. Gibson, Harold A. Greenberg, Bernard H. Hall, Melvin Sabshin, and Robert E. Switzer. Two other members of the Committee, Robert W. Hyde and Fred Robbins, participated in the formulation of the report prior to their transfer to a Contributing Member status.

FOREWORD

For the past decade, a group of psychiatrists, psychiatric nurses, and psychiatric aides has been studying and exploring the nursing care of patients, with the conviction that patient care can be improved, the improvement can be facilitated by increased clinical competence, and supervision of clinical experience will foster increased competence. The psychiatrists are members of the Committee on Psychiatric Nursing of the Group for the Advancement of Psychiatry and the nurses and aides are consultants to the Committee.* As a study group they have shared experiences gained from a wide variety of clinical settings. This publication presents the results of their deliberations.

The study group has worked during a very exciting period in the history of psychiatry and nursing. Throughout this decade there have been many substantial efforts to study and improve the quality of care as mental hospitals have progressed from custodial to treatment centers. This change has served to emphasize the singular importance of nursing personnel in the recovery process of the mentally ill.

GAP Report No. 22, THE PSYCHIATRIC NURSE IN THE MENTAL HOSPITAL, formulated by the Committee and pub-

---

* The Committee on Psychiatric Nursing (see Page vi for listing) wishes to express its deep appreciation to the many consultants who have participated in the deliberations which have led to the publication of this guide. They are: BARBARA B. BUCHANAN, R.N., School of Nursing, University of Florida; FRANCES LENEHAN, R.N., Massachusetts Department of Mental Health; IDA JEAN ORLANDO, R.N., Assistant Professor, and Director, Mental Health Program, School of Nursing, Yale University; HILDEGARD E.PEPLAU, R.N., Ed.D., School of Nursing, Rutgers University; HELEN SAINATO, R.N., School of Nursing, St. Elizabeths Hospital, Wash., D.C.. GORDON SAWATZKY, R.N., Menninger Foundation; WILLIAM THOMAS, P.A., and GWEN TUDOR WILL, R.N., both of Chestnut Lodge, Maryland; and representing the National League for Nursing, KATHLEEN BLACK, R.N.. ELEANOR FRANY, R.N., R.N., JOHN V. GORTON, R.N., and MARY LISTON, R.N.

lished in 1952, was a survey of educational programs for psychiatric nursing personnel. GAP Report No. 33, THE THERAPEUTIC USE OF THE SELF, was formulated by the Committee and published in 1955. This report described manifestations of psychological illness, furnished a theoretical framework for clinical practice, and suggested patterns of appropriate patient care. Demand for THE THERAPEUTIC USE OF THE SELF has steadily continued since its publication. Responses to the report have tended to confirm certain convictions held by the Committee while the report was being written, and strengthened since that time. These are:

• The report had applicability and interest for a considerably broader field than that encompassed by the nursing services alone. This field includes particularly the allied health professions, rehabilitation services, and psychiatric residents.

• The usefulness of the report could be enhanced by amplifying the theoretical constructs with illustrative clinical examples.

To this end, THE THERAPEUTIC USE OF THE SELF has been clarified and revised to keep it abreast of current thinking in psychiatry and psychiatric nursing, and now constitutes Part I, "Theoretical Basis," of the present publication; to this has been added a series of case studies, constituting Part II, "Clinical Application."

The title of the present publication embodies the ultimate objective of these efforts.

(PART ONE)
THEORETICAL BASIS

THEORETICAL BASIS

I. INTRODUCTION

Therapeutic effectiveness in day-by-day nursing care depends upon nursing personnel's* understanding the patient's behavior and responding to it appropriately. This report deals with some psychiatric concepts which we hope will lead to sounder understanding of the patient's behavior. Understanding should lead to clearer recognition of the patient's emotional needs and better corrective responses to them. These concepts are discussed as current working formulations and a dynamic orientation is offered for persons, by whatever title designated, who participate in the daily 24-hour care, treatment, and rehabilitation of the mentally sick. The formulations and examples can be extended and applied to the fields of occupational therapy, physiotherapy, recreational therapy, vocational counseling, volunteer services, and other fields.

We hope that these concepts will be translated into daily action and thus will help the supervisor, teacher, or administrator to make his job assignments, conferences, and classes more purposeful. We also hope that this document will be useful to those concerned with instruction of professional nurses, practical nurses, psychiatric aides, attendants, psychiatric technicians, child care workers, orderlies, workers in the field of rehabilitation, and others who perform similar

---

* The terms *nursing personnel* and *nurse* are used throughout the text to include all persons, whatever their titles, who are involved in the 24-hour care of the mentally sick patient.

1

duties. All of these persons give direct patient care and are well aware of the complexity of human relationships. Too often these relationships are left anxiously unscrutinized. As a result the response and care may be anti-therapeutic.

A patient enters a psychiatric hospital because he has experienced difficulties in living which included a breakdown in relationships with other people. We assume that the behavior of the patient has meaning; that his behavior affects the behavior of those who care for him; and that the behavior of those who care for the patient affects him. The hospital must serve as a smaller world wherein new experiences in living and new personal relationships produce minimal anxiety and maximal support. Thus, the patient gradually may learn to feel that living with others is a less threatening and a less foreboding experience.

The patient's hospitalization should enable him to live more effectively with other people. Every mental illness includes the problem of the patient's particular way of relating himself to others and participating with others in activities. When a patient enters a mental hospital he has already established patterns of behavior to defend himself against anxiety-provoking relationships. Many of these defenses are pathological. In the attempt to cope with his anxiety, the patient chooses that form of expression which, in his past experience, has been most effective in maintaining distance from others for his subjective comfort.

In the hospital new personal relationships must gratify the patient's needs, facilitate his communication with others, and enhance his social participation. It follows that the nursing personnel, who have the longest and most intimate contact with the patient are deeply involved in these processes. Every contact with the patient, whether in the performance of "official nursing care" or in a less directed capacity, involves patient-nurse relationships. The relationship can be therapeutic or harmful. If these relationships remain essentially thera-peutic, they can become an integral part of the patient's whole therapeutic regimen. It is important for nursing per-sonnel to understand and to be aware of the feelings, thoughts, and actions of the patients. They should have a similar un-derstanding of their *own* thoughts and actions in any situa-tion. Such awareness is acquired gradually. It depends upon repeated experiences with patients and the collaborative ex-amination of these experiences with physicians, supervisors, and co-workers.

To enhance awareness of anxiety and of reactions and de-fenses to anxiety, we shall first discuss the theme of *regres-sion* with signs of dependency which is part of every illness, mental and physical; second, we shall consider essential areas of dysfunction; and, finally, we shall re-examine the *changes in relationships* that invariably ensue when chronic and in-tense dependency are expressed.

These phenomena are readily available for continued observation in daily behavior. They are manifestations about which society has ideas of "normality," concepts of good and bad, and of morality and immorality. They raise problems, the mastery of which are the concern of patient as well as nurse.

Nursing personnel and physicians have different primary areas of responsibility and different techniques. It cannot be sufficiently emphasized, nevertheless, that all persons who work with patients must face, and react constructively to, their behavior and the manifestations of regression and altered capacity for human relationships.

The recognition of these processes and the understanding of their dynamic significance can become a common denom-inator of all the different "therapies" to which the patient is exposed. Understanding of these processes offers a basis for communication among the various participants in patient

3

care. Such communication in the hierarchy of personnel provides consistency and direction for the total therapeutic regimen. Moreover, understanding of these concepts should further facilitate the definition of different roles for personnel, and of the various levels and areas wherein each person can best make his contribution toward a plan of treatment.

It should be noted that the case studies illustrating a representative group of daily occurring clinical problems are not intended to offer definitive prescriptive models or techniques for solution of problems. Such an attempt could lead only to premature closure rather than to exploration of feelings and ideas. It is intended that the cases should serve to stimulate discussion and independent thinking. As they are analyzed they will: (1) reemphasize the already generally accepted concept of how nurses' feelings influence the quality of patient care; (2) highlight the importance of open communication among all personnel; and (3) emphasize the importance of adequate supervision. To illustrate significant and commonly occurring clinical problems we chose dramatic situations. A preponderance of these involve unsuccessful approaches.

We are describing a method for ongoing clinical practice. The nature of the patient's illness determines the treatment program. In order to get all relevant facts, treatment planning involves adequate communication at all levels; all personnel must contribute. Conferences, discussions, and supervision will result in ongoing constructive reassessment of the treatment. As the patient changes, treatment changes, and as treatment changes, the individual contributions change. It is hoped that the selected illustrations of clinical problems will be a useful stimulant for supervisors and students in carrying out their own therapeutic programs.

II. REGRESSION WITH
SYMPTOMS OF DEPENDENCY

Regression may be defined as a return to earlier (childhood) methods of solving personal conflicts. It may occur when physical or emotional stress is too severe to be integrated. Everyone, at one time or another, finds the need to return to earlier modes of behavior. For instance, sleep is the universal form of regression following the tiring activities of the day. Often, under the influence of group situations, an individual may allow himself to act in a way that is regressive in nature; an example is the mischievous, childlike behavior frequently observed at a class reunion or at a business convention.

To understand the process of pathological regression, it is necessary first to understand the effects of *progression*, as manifested in the growth toward maturity in the formative years. The infant is endowed with capacities, instincts, and drives that propel him steadily toward growth, development, and maturity—physical and emotional. The normal development of this process can be envisioned as a complex progression. Various stages of development are clearly recognizable in the maturation of the organism.

However, at any time during the course of that maturation the individual may find himself faced with insurmountable conflicts. To cope with the anxiety produced by these conflicts, and despite his propensity for growth, the individual may utilize the patterns of an earlier level of behavior

5

by which he feels more protected and, therefore, safer. This return to earlier modes of behavior is the characteristic of regression.

The more profound the regression, the more childish and infantile will be the patient's behavior. The depth to which he regresses will depend on a number of variables such as the intensity, duration, and severity of the present conflict, the nature of the conflicts which he has faced during his maturation, and the similarity between the conflicts experienced by him as a growing child and as an adult. Following are examples of the operation of each of these variables:

(*a*) The soldier in combat, overwhelmed by fear, fatigue, hunger, and low morale may regress to very primitive modes of behavior. These may be characterized by inattention to basic physical needs. He may lie mute and disinterested in his surroundings.

(*b*) An individual who in childhood suffered from chronic anxiety caused by inordinate demands for performance enters into a relatively benign work situation. Intellectually, he has the capacity to perform this job successfully. Because of his chronic anxiety and his fear of failure, he constantly seeks reassurance from his employer. At home he demands special attention, and sleeps a great deal.

(*c*) A man who as a child felt unloved and deprived of essential emotional relationships may react to a minor rejection, such as a girl friend's refusal of a date, by behavior including temper tantrums, crying, or petulance.

When regressive behavior appears, the individual, though an adult, will seem childish. His usual mature ways of handling problems will be changed. Instead, he will come to depend increasingly on others. He will become indecisive and will expect undue care and attention both physically and emotionally. He will refuse responsibility, or when he at-tempts to deal with problems he will do so inadequately. Fol-lowing are two clinical examples of such behavior:

(*a*) The patient hospitalized for a minor surgical pro-cedure has an uneventful post-operative course. However, on the day he is able to be ambulatory, he says he cannot get up and rejects the nurses' attempts to help him. Dur-ing the next several days, he repeatedly rings the bell and refuses to help himself in any way. It is important to understand this behavior (regression) as a response to the patient's anxiety.

(*b*) On the ward one observes a carelessly dressed, un-shaven patient. He never washes, shaves, or changes his clothing unless the nurse reminds him to do so and assists him. He seems unable to make the most minor decisions for himself. He repeatedly asks the nurse for favors. Yet, before his illness this patient was a fastidious, self-sufficient business executive.

The degree of regression and the accompanying de-pendence may vary from a simple increase in demands for physical care to complete dependence for the most basic functions such as eating or control of bowel and bladder.

Thus far we have stressed regression and dependence as if they occurred in pure form. However, as in any disease, the patient attempts in some way to overcome or deny the occurrence of the process. As a result other responses are set in motion. These are in the form of mechanisms that attempt to hide from others and from himself the severity and type of disturbance that is taking place. We may have, then, the type of reaction in which the individual simply seeks oblivion from the presence of the process. This is simple *denial*. On the other hand, the person may go one step further than simple *denial* and impute the dependence to someone else. This is *projection*. Or, again, he may attempt to cope with the conflict by using actions and expressions that are contradictory and thus ineffective in solving the problem. This is *reaction formation*. In some instances, the person is able to function fairly well by becoming aggressive in helping or in caring for others as he would like to be cared for. In this way he may overcome somewhat successfully the anxiety-provoking process. This is *over-compensation*.

At times, it becomes necessary to respect and support the defense and to make it operable as such. At other times, it is more useful to help the patient face that which the defense is against. For example:

(*a*) A group of patients is going out to a dance. At the last minute, Mrs. Smith, a frightened new patient, complains of a headache, says she feels cold all over, and returns to her bed. Although the nurse recognizes these sudden physical complaints as a defense against this patient's fear, she responds supportively by covering the patient, getting a hot water bottle, and staying with her.

(*b*) Two weeks later, when Mrs. Smith has become adjusted to the hospital, she develops sudden physical complaints when the nurse is taking her to a dance. This time, the nurse, feeling that the patient's defenses no longer needed the same kind of support, helps the patient identify the source of the anxiety and then encourages her to attend the dance.

After the decision has been made either to support the defense or to face the anxiety (never a complete either-or proposition), an estimation of the degree of support and timing of support is also necessary. There must be a readiness to modify degree and timing. For example:

8

(*a*) A patient with a mild degree of dependence may require support until he is able to accept more responsibility.

(*b*) A patient with a moderately severe problem of dependence may need gratification of the dependence by
one nurse while other members of the team may help him
gain insight.

(*c*) A patient with severe problems of dependence may
require the nurse's tolerance of complete regression
through understanding support and love over a long
period of time.

The patient may withdraw from participation in living by
regression and symptoms of dependency. This prevents his
having many experiences that would contribute to strengthening relationships with people. For example, the patient may
refuse to eat, bathe, or dress by himself, and he may become
completely dependent on nursing staff for physical survival.
The nurse may easily assume the role of a person on whom
the patient is dependent, and the patient may come to feel
comfortable when fed, bathed, and dressed. The nurse must
understand why this kind of participation is a comfortable
one for the patient; she must also be aware of her own feelings about having someone dependent upon her. Otherwise,
she may be uncomfortable about giving the sort of care
which may be helpful to the patient at this point in his illness. This involves some understanding of the patient's past
experiences which have necessitated his dependence, and
also some understanding of her own feelings about dependence.

A serious problem may arise when the nurse actually re-
ceives a great deal of satisfaction from working in a situation
in which the patient is dependent on her.[1] In such instances,
the behavior of both may become stalemated at this point;

[1]*See Case No. 15, page 74*

9

the nurse actually fosters this dependent behavior. Such a premium on dependence delays patient recovery. Many cues will be missed that might lead to more independent behavior. The patient may reach for the spoon to feed himself, and the cue not be observed or used. The necessity to maintain the patient's dependence reflects, then, the nurse's need for satisfaction and security, and discourages the patient's first timid attempt away from dependence. The nurse's need to help may keep the patient helpless. Sometimes the greater ease of caring for dependent patients, as a practical matter, makes it difficult for the nurse to support the independent strivings of the patient.

III. AREAS OF DYSFUNCTION

The five areas of dysfunction discussed in this chapter illustrate various mechanisms involved in personality change. These areas of dysfunction of the personality are associated with the ever-present regression and dependence and concomitant disturbed relationship to other persons.

Diminished Integrative Capacity

Every person has some ability to act with a sense of control within himself. This sense of control arises from the maintenance of an equilibrium between the basic impulses and controlling forces. The process involved in this effort toward harmony we shall call integration. Some of the forces within the individual are of a primitive and ruthless nature. They seek gratification in a selfish manner. If the forces were left unleashed, the person would tend toward disintegration. Such threats against others would evoke retaliation.

These forces are restrained early in a person's life. Prohibitions and limitations, primarily through parental attitudes, oppose the wishes for primitive gratification. It is the struggle between the inner desires and the prohibitions (by other persons or, later, self-imposed) that is sensed as conflict. Integration deals with the factors that implement mastery of the ensuing tensions.

The development of mastery begins in early life. It demands a gradual and appropriate weaning from the early feeling of power (omnipotence). The feeling of power is gradually relinquished under the supporting experience of obtaining satisfaction, of being loved and approved. Guidance that sets up pertinent limitations is essential and helps the child survive the ensuing struggle-for-power period of the first years of life. Gradually, a feeling of personal self-strength (ego-strength) is developed which is implemented as the child is helped to delay immediate gratification in favor of long-term pleasurable experiences. He learns to:

- make decisions
- accept disappointment and frustration
- tolerate varying degrees of anxiety
- engage in re-evaluation of standards arbitrarily imposed upon him
- refine reality-testing

The development of ego-strength brings with it an ability on the part of the individual to meet stresses and strains in such a way that they are integrated into the fabric of his personality. However, integration is never complete, nor is the integrative process ever static.

In the course of life all individuals have disruptive experiences sufficiently intense or prolonged to threaten temporarily their personal integration. Repeated experiences of trial and error, of satisfaction and disappointment, leave residues of old conflicts. New situations that cannot be mastered may thereby recall feelings of anxiety attached to these residues and thus may reactivate the earlier conflict and may decrease one's ability to relate to others.

The individual whose capacity for integration is currently intact can meet the ordinary stresses of day-to-day experience without undue anxiety or loss of equilibrium. For instance, a friend's sarcastic or angry remark will be resented briefly, but before long it will be recognized as a sign of irritability or of momentary jealousy and will be replied to either in kind or with friendly tolerance and soon will be forgotten.

Often a patient is not able to integrate experiences or feelings in accordance with learned patterns of behavior. He will participate on the ward in a less adequately integrated manner. For example, he may become confused, doubtful, hesitant, and afraid. If these feelings continue, they alter the patient's perception of the personnel. His resultant behavior towards the staff may evoke fear, doubt, hesitation, and hostility in return. This reciprocal response makes the nurse guilty and anxious about the patient. In extreme situations, the nurse may withdraw from the patient. The understanding of the nurse's feelings about problems of reciprocal integration requires exploration and clarification.[2]

Disturbance of the Function of Reality Testing

One of the most important examples of personality dysfunction is the impairment of reality-testing. In the infant there is little ability to recognize which sensations are coming from outside himself and which sensations originate from within. He is unable to recognize the boundaries of his own body. The environment is perceived as an extension of himself. As the child grows, he learns to delineate himself from his environment.

We may recognize varying degrees of impairment. These may include a severe disintegration in which impaired reality-testing may be expressed by the patient's conviction that he is influenced by magic or electrical forces. In less severe disruptions, the patient may be unable to rid his mind of disturbing, unrealistic fears or obsessive thoughts. The well-integrated normal person under stress may misinterpret other people's attitudes and intentions.

[2]See Case No. 1, page 35   13

Impairment of reality-testing may be perpetuated by a variety of defenses. These defenses prevent the patient from seeing things and people as they really are. His feelings and perceptions do not accurately reflect external reality. These defenses may include *denial,* when the patient maintains that a dead person is not dead; or *distortion,* when the patient regards friendly persons as hostile; or *evasion,* when the patient seems quite unaware of a disturbing reality. Impairment of reality-testing follows the inability of a person to tolerate without serious loss of self-esteem, a reality which is threatening or unsatisfying.

As a patient regresses he may experience difficulties in testing the validity of his perceptions. One patient may, as a result, appear unable to care for himself, while another may be unrealistically confident that he needs no help. Still another may create in fantasy a situation which does not exist, as in delusions and hallucinations.

The effort of the patient to create his own world, frequently without consideration of his family and community, provokes hostile, anxious retaliation from family and community, which may necessitate removal from community and hospitalization.

A hospital provides a more tolerant, protective environment than the disturbing, anxiety-provoking situation from which the patient comes. When a patient is extremely uncomfortable or anxious in his relationships with people around him, he may perceive ward situations and people on the ward quite differently from what they are in reality. The patient's protective or defensive reaction creates a distance between him and people around him, and tends to decrease his discomfort and anxiety. This temporary loss of reality-testing leads to a fantasied relationship with the people around him. For example, a patient can distort the ward situation so that he believes all people to be against him. He can hear them talking about him, and he may then become involved in listening to these people. He must protect himself against them, and thus withdraw to a marked degree from real contact with people in his daily living on the ward.

The nurses, who are in reality part of the people around him, may be made uncomfortable by the patient's expressions regarding nurses' plans to do away with him. They may be so disturbed by their own discomfort that they may stay farther and farther away, and thus reinforce the patient's anxiety. Such a situation makes it difficult to focus on the real problem of how to provide an opportunity for experiences through which the patient does not feel so uncomfortable, and through which reality can gradually return.

Change in Conventional Attitudes and Moral Standards

One way of securing approval and love is by being "good." When this pattern of behavior is the only available one in maintaining relationships the cost is high. Self-expression, creativity, and growth suffer. The person who pays this price often comes to harbor intense resentment against those who seem to demand the "good" patterns. He may rebel against convention itself. For him, direct expression of resentment is not possible as it may bring further disapproval and loss of love. Resentments and fears find expression in behavior which deviates markedly from what is usually considered "proper" or acceptable. It is behavior that usually has a retaliative quality, and may contain an implicit bid for punishment or control.

Respect for moral standards and conventional attitudes expresses itself in conformity. Reasonable social conformity is a compromise between a person's need for affection and an inherent urge for immediate gratification. The need for

15

parental affection is the young child's most fundamental incentive toward socialization. In later childhood, incentive to social conformity also involves the desire for the respect of one's peers. The struggle ordinarily reaches its peak and resolution in adolescence. In the course of the struggle there are rapid shifts between over-conformity and rebellion. Anxiety and insecurity which are part of this conflict may lead to attention-gaining behavior. Such behavior often rejects moral standards and conventional attitudes of the loved ones. Attention-getting tendencies are a means of fulfilling a common childhood need, yet may evoke punishment and threats which, in turn, lead to increased resentment. A conflict ensues: resentment versus a desire for affection.

Some handle the conflict by excessive filial obedience which insures affection and approval. On the other hand, there are often periods of open resentment and a flouting of standards. Symptoms reflecting changes in moral standards and conventional attitudes deal essentially with the mechanisms of distortion, denial, and displacement. These are generally ineffective defenses that try to reduce dissatisfactions experienced in being inadequate, and resentments associated with feelings of lack of affection. The distortions may vary in degree, harbor elements of make-believe, and in their severest form appear as delusions and hallucinations. The resentments translate themselves into a "don't mind, don't care" attitude which then sanctions defiance of standards and conventions. These mechanisms expressed in asocial, amoral, anticonventional behavior become a difficult problem to the patient, as his already handicapped ability to relate effectively with others will now be additionally threatened by disapproval, contempt, or open retaliation. The nurse, however, has the opportunity to assess the implication of this behavior and can avoid adding fuel to the fire.

Such conflict and anxiety is often demonstrated on the hospital ward by a change in the patient's moral standards and conventional attitudes. The patient may refuse to conform to any routine or control. He may be insulting, disrespectful of others, distort the truth, become boastful, and tell tall tales. The patient casts the nurse into an unloving and ungiving role. This is the way he viewed people in the past. When this happens successfully all the resentment is displaced onto those caring for him, and they may be sorely tried in accepting this as illness rather than willfulness.

In the setting of symptoms of *acted-out* resentment, distortion, or denial, the patient usually finds himself in a recurrent state of helplessness. In spite of feeling helpless, the patient is compelled to use the very same or similar defenses which in the first place made him feel inadequate and ineffective. He may be chagrined or embarrassed about it and strives to minimize his helplessness by brazenly flaunting appeals made to him for appropriate behavior. The conflict may result in regressive behavior.

The nurse's response to the patient's behavior can very seriously affect the patient's care. For example, she may become so uncomfortable that she withdraws and gets overly involved in other duties. On the other hand, the patient's actions may provoke a punitive response. Overt forms of counter-aggression may be expressed by the inappropriate use of packs and isolation. In a more subtle way punitive disapproval may be conveyed by gesture, facial expression, and the spoken word. All of this may tend to perpetuate the patient's defiance. Thus the nurse may unwittingly provoke the patient to further defiance.[3] Again, understanding will be greatly facilitated by group experiences in which personnel can compare their experiences with those of others and become aware of their own feelings.

[3]*See Case No. 3, page 39*

Inability to Control Basic Impulses

At the time of birth the child's energies are released by a constant discharge of varied and random impulses, as in the apparently purposeless movements of the muscles of the body. Any minor frustration evokes massive impulsive responses; the crying of the baby involves his entire musculature. Again, when the bowels are filled, the baby responds immediately by evacuation. Hunger is responded to with desire for immediate gratification associated with a crescendo of crying.

In the process of growth the individual learns to control his impulses. To gain love and approval he learns to postpone immediate gratification of such impulses as eating, evacuation of bowels and bladder. He learns that responses to minor frustrations by violent temper outbursts bring disapproval and, therefore, for these and other reasons, he institutes controls. With the emergence of the sexual impulses the process is repeated. By these experiences, he learns to delay gratifications in accordance with the wishes of people with whom he lives and in keeping with the demands of society.

Because of the regression inherent in illness, there is a re-emergence of these basic impulses. The learned patterns of control diminish in varying degrees. The patient may seek immediate impulse gratification. If he is hungry, he demands food. If he is frustrated, he may respond with violent temper tantrums. He may void, soil, and smear on the ward, when and where the impulse emerges.

The patient may respond to loss of control by attempting to mobilize a variety of defenses. One example is the patient who when faced with sexual impulses beyond his control believes that those around are making sexual approaches to him, or that voices tell him to masturbate.

Another more direct solution for the patient is to partic-

18

ipate on the ward in such a manner that he forces the nursing staff to place controls on him. For example, he may constantly tear off his clothing, and as a consequence of his nudity get himself confined to his room. He may become so combative during his rages that his behavior must be physically controlled. His lack of bladder and bowel control leads to being dealt with as a young child during toilet training. The patient thereby gets the nurse to help him control his impulses.

Another method of coping with this problem is evident in the patient who vigorously denies his impulses. The intensity of the denial gives a clue to the strength of the impulses being denied. The loosening of inhibitions and the inability to control impulses which may accompany illness compound the emotional disturbance. The whole process shakes the patient's confidence and security. The emerging anxiety is seen often as a fear of some impending disaster such as death or loss of control. The patient may try to hide these extreme fears, but usually gives clues to them in his actions. He may displace the anxiety to things or situations in the immediate surroundings that seem to justify such emotions. Anxiety arising from fear or loss of control may lead to panic. The demands for frequent contact with the physician or nurses are efforts at alleviation of the anxiety.

The threat of loss of control of impulses, especially those that might call for aggressive action toward others, may lead to anger. Anger, also, may come as a result of disappointment with the staff. It is often closely related to or intertwined with anxiety because the patient fears his own aggressiveness. Hostility is readily recognized. In a more disguised manner, it may be directed inwardly, and the patient may come to hate himself. For example, the loss of a loved one may be accompanied by anxiety and hostility. The patient may show his feelings by criticizing the loved one, or by

19

condemning himself as an unworthy individual—the patient becomes *depressed*. Anxiety and hostility may break through in the form of agitation and rebellion against those near him—against rules, regulations, and reason.

The patient's inability to control his impulses may present difficult nursing problems and may stimulate many negative responses. The patient may refuse to dress in what is considered appropriate clothing. A female patient may allow her blouse to fall open in such a way as to expose her breasts. She may act toward the nurse in a very seductive manner, or may withdraw to a corner of the ward and indulge in open masturbation. Such behavior makes comfortable relationships very difficult. Even though it may be looked upon as the patient's attempt to gain some love and attention from others, nurses may experience great difficulty in maintaining any sort of relationship with the patient if this behavior is not acceptable to them. Here the understanding and awareness of their feelings toward their own basic impulses is significant.

Free discussion about this sort of behavior rather than focusing on its "rightness or wrongness" will enable personnel to handle these problems more intelligently. Their anxiety and discomfort in such a situation does much to sustain this behavior in the patient. When expressed fairly openly, the personnel's discomfort decreases, and the patient may be helped to deal with this problem in a more effective and mature way.[4]

Disturbance of Productive Activity

The process of growth and development requires considerable energy. In infancy the energy requirements are great, since the infant must grow. As growth progresses and becomes slower, there is increasingly more energy available for the use in productive activities. In the adult there is

[4]*See Case No. 18, page 79*

enough available energy so that some can be transmitted to others in the form of physical, emotional, or intellectual support. Energy is also available for productive, creative, and procreative activity.

When conflicts are met in life-situations a certain amount of energy is used in the attempt to solve them. This energy must be drawn from that which normally would be used for productive activity. A patient who is in frequently recurrent conflict uses large amounts of energy in attempting to solve his problems. It follows, then, that there will be very little, if any, energy available for productive activity. In extreme situations the patient may appear stuporous. The regressed schizophrenic is using much energy attempting to solve problems in fantasy.

In the other instances, we may see a patient who participates somewhat in ward activities but soon tires. This is quite apparent in the depressed patient who spends much time with internal struggle and in whom expenditure of effort is followed by almost complete exhaustion. On the other hand, a patient may be using large amounts of energy in what seems to be productive activity, but on closer examination it becomes apparent that he is attempting to deny the presence of internal conflicts by a façade. Behavior of this type is most commonly seen in the manic patient whose defense against conflict is constant activity in which many projects are started—and abandoned. Once the nurse has recognized that she is dealing with an energy disturbance due to conflict she will accept fatigue as a consequence of conflict, not as laziness. She will respond to excessive demands without irritation and resentment.

IV. DECREASED CAPACITY
FOR MATURE RELATIONSHIPS

Some form of emotional interchange with others is characteristic of human beings. The interchange, which is not exclusively verbal, depends also on gestures, facial expressions, tears, laughter, and more subtle physical signs such as turgor of skin, tone of voice, brightness of eyes, blushing, sweating, and posture. These compositely reflect the individual's emotions. Feelings of anxiety, fear, anger, contentment, gaiety, calmness, and puzzlement can be discerned. The recognition of some of these emotions is easy; others require more sensitivity to grasp. It is of utmost importance to learn to recognize unusual, peculiar, conflicting, ineffective, and seemingly purposeless ways of expression.

Emotional interchange between people is motivated by a need to express oneself, to reduce inner tensions, and to obtain a response from the other person. This response is important, since it leads either to gratification or frustration. When an anticipated gratifying response does not occur, the relatively healthy person can decide whether the reason is that he has not made himself understood or that the other person could not respond appropriately. After making such an evaluation, he may try a different approach. The results of trial and error gradually develop the ability to grasp accurately the effect of one's own emotions on another.

The process is complicated. Conscious rational feelings occur simultaneously with unconscious irrational feelings and expressions of these feelings. It becomes clear that this complex interplay between individuals requires personal integration, and leans heavily on intact ability for reality-testing. It demands control of basic impulses. Moral and conventional attitudes of the given cultural and social milieu are reflected also in this process.

Normal development of the capacity for emotional interchanges with other people follows a complex, uneven, hazardous progression. This progression can be divided arbitrarily into three periods in the individual's development:

First comes the early, completely dependent (biological and emotional) infantile period when the need to receive appropriate recognition and gratification is very high. The means of deriving satisfaction or countering frustrations are diffuse and undifferentiated, and at the mercy of the outside world.

Later, a capacity for cooperation begins to develop. The response to frustration during this period can be expressed as active aggression, attack, nonconformity, refusal, withdrawal, or opposition. Satisfaction can be registered in words, compliance in behavior, outbursts of loving affection, and many other ways. This is a period of tentativeness wherein the strength of needs can quickly dispel the cooperative.participating efforts.

In a still later period, the individual develops a more reciprocal emotional participation with others. Empathy with the needs and feelings of others modifies to some extent the demands made on others. Anticipations and expectations become more accurate. A subtle balance between obtaining and providing gratification is achieved. This period deals repetitiously with testing out the internal and external appropriateness of expression of feelings and the responses obtained. The relatively objective assessment of this interplay is an evidence of maturity. At best, there is unevenness, success, and failure for every person. Even to the most mature come experiences of stress and anxiety, both from within and without. The way equilibrium can be sought and obtained, the time in which this can be accomplished, and the maintenance of relative intactness of the person while he meets these stresses are indices of mental health.

Certain life stresses can impair the individual's capacity to relate with others. Such stresses include severe organic changes resulting from harmful and degenerative forces; severe and continued deprivations such as starvation and exposure to extreme temperatures; disorganization of familiar personal relationships because of death or separation; unconscious revival of unmastered inner conflicts, such as feelings of guilt about unrecognized destructive wishes, or anxiety over unconscious temptations of a sexual nature. Every illness, physical or emotional, decreases the individual's capacity for mature object relationships. Every person makes bids for relationships with others, but the sick person's efforts may be clumsy, bizarre, and inappropriate, and may result in rejection.

A patient's defenses may be such that he no longer can repress thoughts of attacking or killing another person. In coping with the resulting anxiety, he may ascribe these feelings to another person and accuse the other person of his own wishes. Irrational as this is, anxiety is thereby partially reduced and a relationship with another person is attempted. The response of the nurse to this behavior is important. If the nurse responds with hostility or withdrawal, she may reinforce the behavior. If she can understand this behavior as a defense, and if she can clarify her own feelings in response to the patient's aggressive feelings and actions, she is then in the position to take the first step toward helping the patient to become less anxious.

A passive and withdrawn patient may give the impression

25

that he is unaware of his surroundings, and does not care to relate to others. Such an assumption is erroneous. This extreme withdrawal or passivity is the only engagement with people the patient is capable of at this moment in his life. Non-intrusive participation is the first step in altering this pattern of behavior. Nurses may be hampered by their belief that one has to be actively doing something in order to be helpful to a patient[5].

A patient who has regressed to an infantile level has a need to be fed, or to be cleaned after soiling, and this may represent a bid for help, for physical closeness to another, for love and affection, for encouragement. He may desire such responses to offset deep feelings of inadequacy, fear of loss of control of his emotions, and possibly feelings of shame and humiliation. He is frightened and wants reassurance that he will not be abandoned. If, in addition to meeting these needs in an understanding manner, the nurse through repeated experiences with the patient becomes alert to cues that indicate his readiness for a more mature relationship, the patient's anxiety may be diminished. The sick person's emotional reactions give evidence that he is trying to relate to others. Repeated failures may overwhelm the threatened person so as to inhibit the recovery process.

When we come into contact with human behavior that is unfamiliar to us, we are tempted to take the expressions literally, using familiar values. The sick person's attempt to relate to the nurse may arouse anxiety, hostility, fear, or contempt. These emotions evoke defensive attitudes and actions on the part of the nurse. When the patient's primitive and crude expressions threaten to overwhelm the nurse, she may defend herself physically.[6] In other instances, she may become oversolicitous. The patient's provocative sexual behavior may arouse in the nurse responses similar in kind and

[5]See Case No. 15, page 74
[6]See Case No. 13, page 65

intensity.[7] The nurse may become terrified as she becomes more aware that she, too, may have feelings and impulses similar to the patient's.

Conflicts, once well buried, may be revived under the impact of dealing with patients. The more the nurse knowingly defends herself against anxiety aroused by these conflicts, the less chance she has of using the relationship effectively. She may abandon the patient by overemphasizing other responsibilities. She may become overly interested in impersonal treatments such as diets and laxatives, or in time-consuming linen counts. She may argue with the physicians that the patient should have shock therapy and maintain that the physicians do not know what they are doing.[8] She may become angry when the patient does not show his appreciation by getting well quickly. She may discourage the patient from discussing what is important to him. The nurse may fail to carry out working arrangements for the patients. She may not insist on regular schedules or may fail to remind patients of appointments. By such methods the nurse diminishes the likelihood of the development of a therapeutic relationship.

The nurse's awareness of the patient's needs and her increased conviction of her own adequacy in meeting these needs will be reflected in her therapeutic skills. Every day opportunities for the development of these relationships are available through the provision of basic nursing care. The nurse can become aware of the meaning and significance of her very presence in relationship to the patient. The nurse will become increasingly able to carry the responsibility of being the person who conveys strengthening, supporting attitudes to the patient.

[7] See Case No. 8, page 50
[8] See Case No. 4, page 42

(PART TWO)
CLINICAL APPLICATIONS

(PART TWO)
CLINICAL
APPLICATIONS

V. FUNCTION AND THERAPEUTIC
EFFECTIVENESS OF NURSING PERSONNEL

In the foregoing discussion, we focused primarily on the *patient's* reaction and its meaning in the interpersonal relationship. In this discussion the focus is primarily on the *other person* in the relationship. As previously indicated the reaction of the nurse to the patient has direct effect on his progress. In this part, we attempt to analyze some of the reactions experienced by the nurse and their significance in this therapeutic relationship.

The function of the nurse is a complex one that has yet to be fully defined. Her functioning may vary from that of a controlling authority figure to a most permissive one. Traditionally, the nurse, like the physician, has been primarily concerned with facilitating more effective relationships and with utilizing interpersonal skills in the day-to-day care of the patient.

What may interfere with the therapeutic effectiveness of the nurse? The nurse must function in a situation of rapidly changing demands. She works with a variety of patients, with supervisors—nurses and physicians, with other nursing personnel, and with persons of other disciplines. She must work with individuals as well as with groups. She tries to cooperate with people of differing attitudes and responsibilities. The nurse responds to problems in ways which reflect her life experience and educational background. Each nurse has her own unique responses.

How well does she understand the way in which she responds to other people? Everything she says to the patient, everything she does for the patient, every move she makes—her very presence—exerts an influence on his immediate condition. The problem in nursing, then, is the nurse's understanding and utilization of her own natural reactions to other people rather than depending on prescribed or conventional attitudes. The nurse who examines her behavior discovers that her own attitudes, likes, dislikes, and other feelings enter into her every action, whether it be a technical nursing procedure or her very presence in the clinical setting. The nurse should be a therapeutic agent. What a nurse does, as a person, is as important as any other technical skill she may possess. Thus, when she understands her own emotions, her own motivations, and her own way of meeting and solving problems, she can function more effectively.

A patient may respond to a particular approach by a nurse in many different ways. He may react appropriately to her behavior or his response may be incomprehensible because his past life experiences and his present illness cause him to distort his perceptions of the total situation. For example, the refusal of a previously cooperative patient to comply with a nurse's request should not be responded to as an overt rejection. Rather, an assessment of the interaction should be made. In this way the feelings of the nurse about what the patient is communicating with this unexpected response can be more clearly understood. From such a realistic appraisal of the situation and her approach, the nurse should be able to gain further understanding, alter her response in light of this understanding, and thereby respond in a way most helpful to the patient.

To help the nurse in her self-appraisal is an extremely difficult task. Complete self-appraisal would require something approaching a personal analysis. Obviously, this is not

32

possible without individual face-to-face discussion. With this limitation in mind, we evolved an approach that would effectively stimulate the nurse to reexamine the relevancies of her responses to the patient. We decided to use clinical mate- rial which helps to highlight the most common and typical situations to which the nurse must respond.

VI. CLINICAL CASE STUDIES

In the material that follows, a number of clinical nursing problems are presented through illustrative case studies. In each of these cases, an attempt is made to identify the nurse's reaction to the patient's behavior and to show the relation of her response to the degree of therapeutic effectiveness. Out of an accumulation of experiences and a proper working through of such experiences, the nurse will develop the capacity for foresight—the ability to anticipate and predict. In so doing, she should be able to increase her therapeutic effectiveness.

CASE 1. *Withdrawal from the Demanding Patient*

A handsome 21-year-old Latin American student was hospitalized with the diagnosis of paranoid schizophrenia. On the day of admission the patient was dejected and withdrawn but on the second day he became excited, appeared fearful of all personnel and several times shouted out of the window, "Help me! Murder! Murder!"

On another occasion, while personnel were preparing a cold-wet-sheet-pack, he thrust his fist through the window pane. Because of his agitation, "sleep therapy" was prescribed and, since he reacted with violence to male personnel, a female nursing student was assigned to care for him during

35

the sleep treatment. She fed, bathed, and toileted him. Within a week the patient entered into group activities. About this same time the nursing student's assignment on this ward terminated.

The patient's only visitor was his mother, a fashionable and sophisticated woman. Mother and son were exceptionally close and walked down the corridors with their arms around each other. The nursing personnel were surprised to find that on each visit the mother left comic books and lollipops in his dresser drawer.

The patient became increasingly interested in group activities; simultaneously, he gradually became more attentive to the head nurse on his ward, although he rarely spoke to anyone else. One morning while this nurse was sitting with a group of patients, the patient after staring at her for some time said, "I have committed a sin." Following a non-directive technique that she had been taught, the nurse replied, "You have committed a sin?"

"Yes," he stated, "I have eaten my mother, and that is evil".

Glowering at the nurse, he left the room. Uncertain as to what to do next, the nurse decided to remain with the other patients.

The next day the patient began to follow her about the ward. Day after day, he waited patiently and quietly outside the nursing office until she emerged.

He would walk with her, staring intently, sometimes adoringly, and sometimes angrily. One afternoon as she gave him his medication, the patient smiled, looked deeply and intently into her eyes, touched her cheek, and said, "You are a good mother."

Again, the nurse restated his remark, "I am a good mother?"

"Yes".

The nurse reported this incident to the psychiatrist who was noncommittal in his response.

From then on, the nurse never allowed herself to be alone with this patient. Instead, she tried to interest him in group activities on and off the ward. He responded by withdrawal from any further attempts to get close to the nurse, other personnel, or patients.

In this example, when the nursing student was transferred, the patient turned his interest toward the head nurse, bidding for closeness with her and probably indicating what he may have perceived as a quite difficult relationship to his mother. This was communicated to the head nurse in disguised form by fantasies. The head nurse was too uncomfortable, could not accept the patient's movement toward her or utilize it in a way useful to the patient. The patient subsequently withdrew even further from relationships with other people on the ward.

Speculations about the nature of the problems of the head nurse which served as interferences to the progress of this patient must include the impact upon the nurse of having this handsome 21-year-old male patient following her around hour after hour. In addition, there was the disturbing effect of the patient's repeated, "You are a good mother," after having said, "I have eaten my mother". This, when associated with the patient's fluctuation between adoration and anger, aroused disturbed feelings in the nurse.

The head nurse faced a different situation than did the student. She had too many other patients to look after, while the student had only this one. The nurse had insufficient supervised experience in working with this kind of problem; also she was intimidated by the destructive nature of the expression of closeness. The student did not have to face this situation since the patient was in sleep therapy.

Under the circumstances, the nurse could not respond

37

in an appropriate helpful manner to the patient's strong demands.

She could only respond to the patient in a stereotyped, inhibited manner as evidenced by her "non-directive" approach. This was her defense against the stress of the situation; here the "non-directive" approach impaired the therapeutic relationship.

Recognizing her difficulties she went to the physician for help. He, too, was "non-directive." As her attempts to gain support from him were unavailing, she could only withdraw.

CASE 2. *Meeting the Needs of the Over-Demanding Patient*

Mrs. A who had been in the hospital for the past nine months had obtained a reputation for being difficult and a trouble-maker. She was transferred to Ward X, where she rapidly became the center of everyone's attention. She constantly asked the nurses to do things that in their opinion she was capable of doing herself, fetching her glasses from her room, fixing the hooks on her bra, etc. When the nurses refused to comply with her requests she became sarcastic and tried to persuade other patients to refuse medications and in other ways disobey the nurses. The nurses responded by putting her in seclusion and by making requests for her transfer to another ward.

Following a ward staff meeting, it was decided that Nurse M should give this patient special attention. Nurse M agreed to attempt to satisfy all her requests. The other nurses were instructed to do the same when they had time. If they were busy they were to tell the patient so and refer her to Nurse M. The total situation was to be reviewed in one week.

Initially, there was a rapid increase in the patient's demands. This lasted for a few days and then began to diminish. At the same time there was a marked improvement in her behavior. She ceased needling the nurses, ceased provoking the other patients to behave badly, and became relatively cooperative with all the nurses. Her dependency on Nurse M became marked. Initially, when Nurse M was off duty, Mrs. A's behavior would deteriorate. After two months of this regimen, when Nurse M was off duty, the patient became depressed instead of *acting out*. Prior to her relationship with Nurse M the patient was wont to talk loudly with other patients about her sexual relationship and exploits with her husband. Here, too, a marked change took place. The patient became reticent about her relationship with her husband, with everyone except Nurse M to whom she confided her fears about, and disgust for, the sexual act.

It is of interest to note that at no time during this period was the patient seen by any other therapist.

CASE 3. *Bribery Used for Acceptance*

Kathy and Mary were intelligent, attractive, and thoroughly rebellious teen-agers who occasionally took it upon themselves to "test the limits" of the adolescent treatment unit. They reinforced each other in episodes of disruptive behavior and had eloped on three previous occasions. To prevent further elopement orders were written forbidding them to be allowed off the ward together. This order was especially emphasized when the treatment program for these two patients was discussed with the nursing students who received clinical experience on the ward.

The nursing student involved in the following incident was a shy, passive person who could not effectively accept

39

or set limits. During her first two weeks on the adolescent ward she made only a few tenuous patient contacts, such as getting something for a patient or answering a direct question. This behavior contrasted with her ability to do excellent work on the geriatric ward; she had been described by her instructors in the geriatric service as alert, and conscientious, although over-compliant. After the first weeks the psychiatric patients made few requests of her and usually turned to one of the other nurses. She no longer participated in the shop talk of the other students, and had little to say at conferences about the patients.

During the fourth week, Kathy and Mary, separately and together, approached this student on numerous occasions and "permitted" her to do things for them. The student responded enthusiastically and intensified her efforts to comply with their requests until the following incident occurred.

One evening Kathy and Mary asked the student to take them off the ward and down to the lobby for a coke. She hesitated momentarily but acquiesced when Kathy said, "Oh it won't take but a minute. We can be back by the time you ask the head nurse. We knew we could count on you".

As soon as they reached the lobby and got the cokes, they threw them down and bolted for the unlocked door. Surprised and hurt, the student broke into tears and tried to catch them but was prevented by another patient who "playfully" held her until Kathy and Mary were out of sight.

The nurse returned to the ward to report what had happened. The head nurse attempted to utilize this incident to help the student achieve insight into why she had taken the patients off the ward without notifying anyone and had disobeyed the specific order prohibiting their absence from the ward. The student, however, was so overwhelmed with remorse that she could not reflect on her behavior. Paradoxically, she appeared to respond with increased guilt and anxiety to the head nurse's matter-of-fact, non-punitive attitude.

These data emphasize two related themes. First, the student's difficulty in coping with her own rebellious feelings are expressed in her identification with the two adolescents. That she had trouble coping with her rebellious impulses can be inferred from her characteristic over-compliance, her inability to function adequately when she was expected to exert control over patients who exhibited a high level of rebelliousness, and finally her direct impulsive flouting of authority. In contrast, she could function well with geriatric patients since their submission did not stimulate her rebelliousness.

Secondly, because of the adolescent nature of her conflict, she lacked sufficient inner controls and was not yet able to form mature identifications with the staff, her professional role, and its controlling effect on her own impulses. The non-punitive attitude of the staff as she interpreted it provided inadequate external reinforcement. Consequently, she tried to have only a minimum of contacts which remained superficial and tenuous. Avoidance of responsibilities would generate guilt and anxiety in such a conscientious person. Her withdrawal from the patients was followed by withdrawal from the staff and her fellow nurses.

The nurse's anxiety about her inability to relate to the patients expressed her conflict between the need to withdraw and the desire to reestablish herself professionally. Consequently, she was vulnerable when Kathy and Mary attempted to exploit her—especially since the price of their acceptance was only in terms of *doing* things for them. By catering to their requests, she effected an anxiety-alleviating compromise in which, by superficially relating to them and giving them care, she believed that they were accepting her.

The amount of anxiety and insecurity she experienced was directly reflected by her rebelliousness and the man-

41

ner in which she acceded to their demands. Her anxiety was compounded by her own inability to assess the events correctly and the lack of necessary understanding and support from the supervisory personnel. This circular process of anxiety leading to withdrawal from patients and staff resulted in further anxiety and guilt, and culminated in the student's inability to respond to the head nurse's attempt to give her support or to achieve any degree of insight.

It is probable that the conscientious, highly motivated nurse is especially prone to being caught in this kind of dilemma when she is faced with a non-punitive matter-of-fact attitude by a person in authority. One often encounters this type of reaction in response to errors in judgment made early in a psychiatric experience. When supervision can intervene effectively in this process, a further step toward therapeutic use of the self occurs.

CASE 4. *Honesty vs. Hypocrisy*

The remodelling of two wards (A and B) entailed the evacuation of all patients. Owing to uncertainty as to when the maintenance crews were going to start, numerous dates were set for their transfer. As each day for the move came round it was cancelled. The response of the patients on the two wards was quite different. On Ward A, the patients remained stable even though they were annoyed by the repeated changes in dates set for their transfer. On Ward B, six patients became incontinent; there were four fights within a period of one week; a number of patients showed marked increase of psychotic manifestations, hallucinations, and delusions, etc.

On investigating the different responses of the two wards to the same situation, the following difference in nurse behavior was strikingly apparent. On Ward A, the nurses, too, were annoyed by the changing dates. Supported by their supervisor, they made no attempt to hide their annoyance and made it clear to the patients and other staff members that it was in response to administrative indecision. On Ward B, however, the nurses attempted to hide their annoyance and defended, somewhat hypocritically, the administrative vacillation, even when one of the more articulate patients was critical of the indecision. On Ward A, the nurses had maintained their professional relationship with their patients through their honesty in feeling and communication. On Ward B, the patent dishonesty in feeling and communication of the nurses broke the relationship with their patients; hence, the marked increase of regressive behavior and *acting out*.

CASE 5. *The Professional Person as a Patient*

Miss B, a 45-year-old surgical nurse, was admitted to the hospital on a voluntary basis. Her educational preparation included a Master's Degree, but she was retired from professional activity because of her emotional instability.

The head nurse was the only member of the nursing personnel able to establish a therapeutic relationship with the patient. She was not intimidated by Miss B and was able to accept the patient's truculent outbursts. Firm and persevering in enforcing ward regulations, the head nurse was able to remove a razor which the patient had obtained from other personnel contrary to ward policy. She treated Miss B as a patient despite her aggressive and patronizing behavior, but somehow she was unable to help other personnel in utilizing this approach.

The patient's behavior on the ward was characterized by a condescending and patronizing attitude toward the nursing personnel. She frequently criticized the personnel and referred to them as being stupid, lazy, and neglectful of patients. In response to these accusations the nursing personnel increasingly ignored her and permitted her to violate ward regulations.

Miss B's relationships with other patients were characterized by intimidation and condescension. She refused to participate in ward work assignments as she felt they were menial tasks and beneath her. Since she was overbearing and patronizing, the other patients on the ward did her work assignments as well as their own.

The patient was thus controlling her environment by intimidating the patients and all of the nurses except the head nurse. Furthermore, she intimidated the physicians by reporting them to the superintendent as incompetent, and adding a wide variety of other threats.

This illustration presents a common situation wherein a patient is not seen as a patient by psychiatric personnel. The patient's similar age, and professional and cultural background, may threaten the integration of the personnel. As a result, they may react to the threat by perceiving the patient as less sick than the patient really is. The person is not seen as a patient but as a hostile, bullying person.

Unable to maintain objectivity, the personnel recoil from the patient's hostility and participate with the patient in a mutual withdrawal process. The nursing personnel's position is reinforced when the physician is seen by them as being as helpless as they are in the situation.

It would seem that the head nurse's ability to work effectively with Miss B was based, at least in part, upon her ability to view her as a patient. As a result, she was able to be more objective and helpful to the patient than other members of the personnel. Although the head nurse was able to work effectively with the patient, she was unable to assist the ward staff in achieving this objective. The gratification that comes to a professional person from knowing that she is the only one who can work with a given patient may have been a deterring factor in the implementation of a successful nursing care plan. The total treatment plan was apparently not geared to meet the patient's need for a more structured ward environment. The personnel's perception of the patient's needs were distorted because of their involvement in the mutual withdrawal process.

CASE 6. *Placing the Blame*

A young woman was admitted as a transfer from another hospital. In the previous hospital she had been closely supervised because of a severe depressive action, suicidal preoccupation, and a history of suicidal attempts. The self-destructive acts usually came in response to unanticipated separations from significant people and in response to the bickering between her parents or between her husband and her parents. Such bickering invariably distracted attention from her needs. She had little awareness of her contribution to the continuation of these behavior patterns.

In the new hospital, the more ominous depressive symptoms were not apparent, and a fairly permissive privilege program was instituted. Two weeks after admission the patient left the hospital grounds and committed suicide.

The nursing personnel reacted to the news of the suicide with two major responses. First, they made sure that there had been no negligence insofar as "orders" were concerned; no one could put the blame on them. Second, they directly and indirectly placed the blame for the tragedy upon the medical administration and the hospital in general.

The nursing complaint regarding medical administration

45

was both general and specific. The general complaint was that
the recent move towards an "open," "permissive" hospital atmosphere placed a responsibility on both patients and
nurses which was not necessarily therapeutic. They felt that
in a "permissive" atmosphere some self-destructive acts could
not be prevented. Related to this view was their specific complaint about the administrative physician of the unit which
had housed the depressed patient. Personnel stated that this
psychiatrist changed his orders too hastily, was too permissive, and was not available when needed for direction. All
in all, they had felt ignored and helpless in using their independent judgment. As the discussion of this problem continued, it soon became apparent that within the nursing service there was considerable conflict regarding the increasing
autonomy of the nursing department entailed in the responsibilities of a more open hospital. Some nurses said, "We have
to grow into the idea of being autonomous and trusting our
own decisions. If we disagree with an administrator, we have
to talk it out with him. We frequently fall down in setting
limits because we feel we will be criticized by administrator
or therapist."

With the growing awareness of inter- and intra-service
conflict, the wide implications of "placing the blame" became
clearer. The ward administrative physician was quite new to
the hospital, and the senior administrative physician and the
clinical director were not readily accessible because of vacation schedules. They were not able to supply close supervision and support for the ward administrator during this
period of acclimation. Also, during this period of the patient's two weeks at the hospital, the director of nursing was
on vacation and the area nursing supervisor had to extend
her activities. Thus, the key personnel were not available and
this played an important part in the feelings of helplessness
experienced by the nurses. In addition, the more experienced

46

administrative personnel might have diagnosed an impending crisis and taken more appropriate action.

The dissension in the staff closely duplicated the patient's lifelong experience of parental bickering and resultant inattention to her needs. That the nursing service was amply aware of the patient's need for supervision is observed in the comment of the ward charge nurse: "She (the patient) said everything was rosy, and I kept telling her things were not this way. I can't help it if she did come from a hospital where she was under lock and key; it wasn't that much rosier here." The nurse made the pertinent clinical observation that a depressed patient who suddenly, without good reason, begins stating that things are much rosier in a new situation is probably a most serious suicidal risk. During each of the two days preceding the suicide, the patient was permitted unescorted ground visits of ten hours with her mother. The mother was notorious for her belittling and demanding attitude toward her daughter. The patient's need for some protection from this was seemingly ignored.

On the day of the suicide, the charge nurse was off duty. The therapist phoned in sick that morning, and the patient was told he would not be seeing her. The nurse in charge failed to report this information to the nursing office and to the medical administration.

Once again, the patient's needs were not clearly seen even though this separation from charge nurse and therapist directly duplicated for her previous unanticipated separations to which she had reacted by self-destructive attempts. There were no limitations of privileges, no special escorts, even though both such actions can be taken by nursing personnel in emergency conditions. On this score, too, there was for the patient a duplication of adverse life experiences to which she was most sensitive.

For all persons there is increased anxiety and a lessened

ability to express feelings when there is real or imagined lack of clarity in responsibility, authority, and sources of support. Such increased anxiety interferes with constructive awareness of other persons' needs. In an institutional setting, this may result in inadequate care for the patient, and this inadequate care may result in a disaster. The reaction of personnel to a disaster is often very revealing of the stresses and strains within an institution. In this case, the process of "placing the blame" was an attempt to handle an anxiety and guilt-laden situation. When the data became available, retrospective analysis made it clear that several opportunities for therapeutic intervention had been missed. In addition, the situation compounded anxieties already at play and revealed schisms in the institutional structure. Hopefully, the ultimate analysis and resolution of such a hospital-wide crisis leads to a re-evaluation of the therapeutic climate and an increased therapeutic use of self by all personnel.

CASE 7. *Blackmail With "Gifts"*

Mrs. C is a 50-year-old housewife and mother whose present hospitalization occurred after she had presented several neighborhood children and their families with "gifts" of poisoned candy. She felt that they had not accepted her in a friendly manner. Previously, she had been hospitalized following the birth of the first of her two daughters. Her marriage had been incompatible, and her entire life history was one of considerable turbulence.

In the hospital, Mrs. C proved to be a "good patient." Although she was somewhat curious and prying, she had come to be accepted by the staff; this acceptance was, in part, through her numerous gifts of crocheting.

During the Christmas holidays, this woman was an active contender in a contest for the "most originally decorated door." Several of the judges were nursing staff personnel who had been recipients of her "little tokens". One by one, she singled them out and told them that the gifts they had accepted had been made from hospital supplies. The intent to blackmail was little disguised.

Two of the nurses thus confronted became uneasy and assured her of their support. Another angrily went to her supervisor, protesting with chagrin that she had been blackmailed; however, she did not wish to "make trouble". One judge told the patient that he would vote for the door he thought to be the most original. This particular judge was able to discuss the matter further with Mrs. C, reminding her that the staff had not been aware of the source of the gifts and, in general, was able to clarify the realistic factors in the situation. The patient was able to accept this, and her manipulations stopped. Furthermore, she acknowledged her awareness of what was going on and said that she had known the others would be too frightened and would vote for her.

This incident illustrates the need for a knowledge of the motivation of the behavior patterns utilized in order to gain acceptance. Meeting such a patient's manipulative maneuvers is a somewhat simpler task in the light of her previous history and an understanding of the meaning of her many gifts. It is interesting that this was apparently not taken into consideration by many of the personnel, or utilized by them in understanding and in dealing with this particular patient. This may have been, in part, related to the rather frightening nature of the earlier deeds. However, from the theoretical standpoint, this extreme only highlights the general principle involved, namely, the need of the patient to be accepted and the subtly coercive maneuvers to gain this acceptance. The similar origin and meaning of the words *gift* and *poison* is rather nicely substantiated by the dynamics operative in this case.

Another important factor which may be noted in this case has to do with the necessity for an over-all assessment and understanding of the ward situation at the time an incident occurs. It is a well-known observation that childhood sibling rivalries and feelings of rejection by parental figures come into the foreground at the Christmas season. Of course, this is true of personnel as well as patients and may account for an increase in problems during the holiday season.

In this case, as in many instances of *manipulative behavior* in a hospital setting, one of the most appropriate and immediate means of handling the situation is clarification of the reality situation to the greatest extent practical. The judge who was personally most secure was in a position to comprehend, test the situation adequately, and deal with it in a manner that was therapeutic. For whatever reasons, this particular individual was not intimidated by the double-edged meaning of the gift and of the acceptance of the gift.

CASE 8. *The Patient as a Victim*
of Misunderstanding in Supervision

The following clinical observations, demonstrating nurse-patient interaction, were selected from a three-month participation-observation study carried out by a graduate student nurse. The patient was seen by the nurse one hour daily, four days a week. The nurse was supervised by the staff psychiatrist and had frequent conferences with the Director of the Graduate Nurse Program. These observations covered a period of two months, during which the patient talked of running away with increasing frequency. Approximately three weeks later the patient carried out her threat in a way that was quite disturbing to the nurse.

Over a period of one and one-half months, the patient had talked about wanting to go home each time she was seen by the graduate nurse. Most of these comments were countered with the nurse's statement, "You must have permission from our doctor before you can leave the hospital". On a few occasions, the subject was initiated by the nurse: "Do you still think a lot about going home? Why do you think you would like to go home," etc.

The day the patient ran away she was taken, at her request, beyond the hospital limits to a park. A verbatim account of the incident, taken from the participation-observation studies, follows:

> The patient said, "Let's walk on down to the river".
>
> I looked at my watch and said, "I'm sorry, but don't feel we will have any time to go further".
>
> She looked at me with a pained expression on her face and said, "But I don't want to go back. Can't we walk down to the river?"
>
> "I'm afraid that would be a little too far for us to go, and besides, we don't have time."
>
> "I'm not going back," she answered. "I'm going to walk on home now that I'm this far."
>
> "But you'll have to go back, Mrs. D, you can't go home without the doctor's permission."
>
> "No, I'm going home. You go back and I'll see you later." With this the patient got up and hurriedly started off in the opposite direction.
>
> I called as I ran behind her. "Please come back, Mrs. D, and let's go talk to the doctor about going home."

51

She suddenly changed her course and started back towards me, I got the impression she wasn't coming back to me but from the way she was looking around she didn't seem quite sure of the way she wanted to go. As she came past, I caught her by the arm.

She was quiet for a short while as I talked to her. "Mrs. D, you don't want to go home this way. You will only have to be brought back. If you wait until you have the doctor's permission, you can stay for a while and not have to worry about someone coming after you."

With this the patient broke away from me and ran. I followed her to a building where I telephoned the hospital to send some help. I then went out to the road and watched as she ran out of sight. I waited for the hospital car and we then started out to look for her. We quickly found her walking down the railroad track.

During her work with the patient, the nurse had become increasingly anxious about her relationship with the supervising staff psychiatrist. She felt he was not really interested in helping her, and this manifested itself in many ways; questioning her in great detail about her interaction with the patient (which had been recorded for him so that he could read it previous to her appointment with him); spending time during the hour explaining basic concepts of psychiatry which did not seem pertinent to her, etc. She had tried frequently to discuss with him her feelings about escorting this patient on walks because she considered her an elopement risk, and had pointed out the patient's verbalizations which seemed to reinforce this danger. The nurse felt he dismissed this too casually; he made the following statement two days prior to the patient's attempted escape: "D's just talking—she won't go any place. She doesn't have enough energy to walk out the door if it were unlocked. I think you're over-reacting".

Subsequent discussion with the nurse revealed that perhaps she had actually wanted the patient to run away and had encouraged this by taking her to an area considered off-limits by the hospital. She stated that the nursing service personnel on the unit had teased her about the incident and that the supervising psychiatrist had expressed amazement that it had occurred. She still felt very antagonistic toward the psychiatrist for putting her "in that position"; she could not resolve her feelings toward him and, eventually, became overtly hostile to the patient. This outburst was quite unusual for this nurse. She had immediately felt very guilty, anxious, and depressed, and said to the Director of the Graduate Nurse Program the day of the first incident, "I just can't work with this patient any more—she's bound to suffer. All the feeling I have toward the psychiatrist is being displaced onto the patient. I know it, but I can't do anything about it".

In addition to the displaced hostility, a large part of the nurse's resentment toward the patient stemmed from the fact that the patient had in many ways rejected her attempts to form a relationship. The nurse acutely felt a sense of failure, and her rather intellectualized insights about her displaced feelings were at least partially a defense against the anger she felt toward the patient for rejecting her. The patient's *acting-out* in this particular incident appears to have resulted from the anxiety generated by being caught in the middle of the doctor-nurse struggle.

In many ways what happened is similar to the "mirror-image" mechanism described by Stanton and Schwartz[9]. The doctor and nurse were mutually antagonistic and talked past each other. Instead of dealing with their feelings directly, they tacitly agreed to disagree about the patient. On the one hand, the doctor became less concerned about the possibility of elopement (although the patient had done so frequently); on the other hand, he became much more restrictive and withdrew many of the patient's privileges without explanation to either the patient or the nurse. The nurse followed an opposite pattern of becoming increasingly concerned with the problem of escape but going to great lengths to cater to the patient

See bibliographical reference, page 119

by buying her cigarettes and stretching the rules concerning privileges. The patient, caught in this web of compounded inconsistency, perhaps attempted to run away to clarify her status. She did not know that she was a victim of disagreement between the psychiatrist and the nurse but sensed the tension. Her subsequent behavior forced the staff to take definitive restrictive measures.

CASE 9.   *Contrasting Expectations*

Mr. G was a 34-year-old man who had been hospitalized intermittently for many years. At times he was severely disorganized in his thinking, careless about his appearance, and impulsively assaultive. At other times he was in fairly good contact, friendly, and displayed a good sense of humor. Visits by his parents were often disturbing. They hovered over Mr. G, picked at him about minor details of his appearance, and criticized him for overeating. His mother was particularly guilty of this and seemed oblivious to the impact that it had on her son. He frequently became disturbed in her presence and she in all seriousness suggested that it must be because he didn't like the particular type of glasses she was wearing.

During one of his better periods, while on the way to the dining room, the patient passed his psychotherapist and ward psychiatrist in the hall. He smiled at them and then very deliberately continued to walk as though he were going to leave the building rather than go to the dining room. A student nurse who was escorting the patients to the dining room followed him to the front lobby and asked him to return. The patient gave no indication that he was making a serious attempt to leave the hospital and there was plenty of help available should it be needed. The student nurse waved her finger at him and said sharply, "Go right back and get down to the dining room". The patient raised his arm more in a gesture of irritation than as a threat to strike her. The student nurse again shook her finger in the patient's face, saying, "Mr. G, don't you dare raise your hand to me!" At this point the patient struck her in the face knocking her to the floor. He became disturbed, confused, and mumbled incoherently. Only after several days did he gradually emerge from his disturbed state.

The student nurse in this case felt her professional competence threatened by the patient's behavior (especially because of the large audience) and she lashed out vigorously. Unwittingly she had triggered the patient's response by behaving in a way similar to his mother. Contrast her handling of this incident with that of the head nurse when she was faced by a similar situation.

Mr. G was being escorted by the head nurse to an appointment with his therapist. This made it necessary for them to walk a distance of several hundred yards on the grounds. As they started, the patient abruptly changed course as if he planned to leave the grounds. The head nurse stayed with him emphasizing that his psychiatrist was expecting him and that he did not have permission to leave the grounds at this time. Mr. G slowed up a bit but continued towards the front gate. The head nurse repeated the limits saying, "Mr. G, you can't go off the grounds; you have to go to your appointment." He replied to this saying, "Well, it's going to take force." The head nurse, sensing that the patient was not too serious about wanting to leave the grounds and appealing to his sense of humor, said, "Well, *I* certainly can't force you; why don't we go find some aides who can?" Mr. G laughed, walked with the nurse until they found an aide, and went to his appointment without further protest. In this instance the nurse had had greater experience with the patient and was better able to predict his behavior. Perhaps even more important, she did not feel threatened and did not need to react defensively.

The student nurse expected trouble and she got it. The head nurse felt able to handle the situation and she was.

CASE 10. *Myth of the "Dangerous Patient"*
           as Exploited by the Ward Personnel

Mr. E, a short, stocky Irishman, was proud of being considered the most troublesome patient in the entire hospital. He was suspicious, irritable, belligerent, and averaged at least one fight each day. If another patient so much as brushed his arm or dared to use any particular article to which Mr. E had staked claim, he would strike without warning. It was clear to all nursing personnel that Mr. E was deriving a great deal of satisfaction from the attention paid to him. He was all too willing to be "martyred" by being secluded. If he were placed in cuff restraints, he took advantage of the occasion to demonstrate that he could still beat any other patient on the ward by using his feet and forehead. Despite the fact that technically he was a poor fighter and rarely injured anyone except himself, his reputation for being "a very dangerous patient" grew until it acquired the status of fact. Rarely did the morning report fail to highlight one of his outbursts. Few hospital bull-sessions failed to cover the latest gossip about him. In fact, an outside observer would have readily seen that Mr. E consumed an almost unbelievable amount of time and energy of the staff on this three hundred bed unit.

To the new ward doctor, this patient presented the challenge of his then brief career as a psychiatrist. If he could do anything with this patient, "who everybody knew was difficult", his local reputation as a therapist would be assured.

From the beginning, the doctor let it be known that Mr. E was to receive special treatment and privileges. Even in this over-crowded state hospital ward, a private room for the patient was arranged. If the patient did not want to eat in the dining room with the rest of the patients, he was to be served in his room. When Mr. E, in one of his tantrums, kicked in the ward radio, the doctor saw to it that he got his own private radio which could be kept in his room.

The doctor then announced that the patient was to be actively encouraged to verbally express his hostility, and that any time the patient felt angry towards any of the aides, the doctor, the patient, and the aide involved would go into the office and "have it out." This arrangement resulted in an increasing series of incidents in which the patient accused the aide of having struck or kicked him while attempting to break up one of his fights with other patients. The aides viewed the "having it out" sessions as kangaroo courts where the patient took the role of prosecutor, the aide that of the defendant, with the doctor acting as judge—who always found the defendant guilty. The aides retaliated by not only failing in trying to prevent Mr. E from fighting with the other patients but by actually encouraging the more aggressive patients to "stand up for themselves." In the following months, Mr. E's episodes of assaultive behavior increased greatly, and he was injured several times by the aides while they were ostensibly breaking up a fight.

By this time, none of the personnel on the unit was impartial or uninvolved, and a close look at the situation revealed that Mr. E's assaultive behavior was tacitly tolerated, if not actually abetted, by the doctor and the aides.

An observer who entered the ward at the height of the difficulty noted that the emotional reactions of the personnel when reciting their latest trials with this patient did not at all correspond to their account of how much trouble he had

57

caused them. On the contrary, their reactions contained elements of pleasure and satisfaction.

The aides, however, were quite angry at the doctor. The
latter, on the other hand, felt that most of the aides were a
calloused bunch of "bughousers" who could not, or would not,
understand his treatment program. It must be said that the
hospital, at this time, was undergoing extensive reorganiza-
tion and that the doctor's appraisal of some of the aides was
not totally incorrect. As is the case in every attempt to change
a hospital from one of custodial care to an active treatment
center, there was a great deal of sensitivity to anything which
smacked of being "an old-time method"—especially physical
abuse of the patients. The doctor's conscious and unconscious
motivations led him to capitalize on this intolerance of any
rough handling by using the patient's assaultiveness to create
incidents which would permit him to get rid of those aides
who he felt were undesirable.

It is also possible that through his identification with the
patient he achieved some personal satisfaction in being aggressive toward those aides who stubbornly resisted all of his
new ideas about patient management.

In addition to the short-term gain which the doctor derived in achieving his ends through the assaultive behavior
of this patient, there are other more general aspects of the
"dangerous patient myth." It is a commonplace occurrence
for the behavior of patients to be exaggerated far out of pro-
portion and thus to be perpetuated in the verbal tradition of
the psychiatric unit thereby becoming a ward myth. This is
most true for the aides, although occasionally the nurses participate in this fiction. This particular myth of a dangerous
patient creates an atmosphere of tension and potential violence on the ward which serves some of the inner needs of
the personnel which have rarely been made explicit. Inter-
views with the aides on this ward revealed that job prestige

ran on a continuum from infirmary or geriatric unit which was poorly regarded to "this ward" which was highly prized. Examination of these phenomena revealed some of the hidden motives for the exaggeration and the barely covert encouragement of assaultive behavior.

One of these motives was the aide's need for status. All too often the aide feels that in the eyes of others, there is nothing which he can do better than anyone else on the psychiatric team except physically restrain the assaultive patient. Further, he believes that the doctor's and nurse's technical competence in all other aspects of patient care exceeds his, and that his contribution is unique only when *muscle* is required. As a consequence, the aide believes that none but he can cope with the assaultive patient. Status and prestige are then derived from the aide seeing himself in the role of protector of the doctor and the nurse, and as indispensable to their efforts with the patient. On the other hand, aides who feel insecure and resentfully see themselves as being without status or power will often fantasy and talk about letting the assaultive patient be the instrument of their aggression—by allowing him to strike the doctor or nurse. From insights into the folklore of the hospital, attitudes can be detected which tend to foster combative behavior in the patient.

Another and more pathological of these motives which exploit the assaultive tendencies of the patient can be observed in some of the personnel who prefer to work on acute wards with combative patients. An observer can often detect elements of pleasure in the excitement following an emergency caused by an assaultive outburst. This is most clearly seen in those of the personnel who must make the greatest struggle to control their own aggressive tendencies.

Such personnel tend to externalize their inner conflicts by

59

projectively attributing them to patients; then, by vigorously
suppressing combative behavior between the patients, they are
in a sense reassured of their own self-control. In addition,
they strike a posture of hyper-vigilance and react to a slight
scuffle as though it were a serious assault. These attitudes
and behavior communicate a feeling of tension to the patients
which set in motion assaultive impulses.

There is another common situation in which the staff uses
one patient to give vent to its hostility toward another patient.
This often occurs when the ward personnel are in disagreement with each other about the management of a troublesome patient. For example, there is the patient who is "into
everything" and continuously exhibits provocative behavior
such as taking things which belong to other patients, stopping
up lavatories, etc. If adequate management devices are not
agreed upon, the ward personnel often find themselves in an
ambiguous position, and their frustration generates hostility
toward the patient. In such circumstances, it is not rare for
an aide to remark, "Just wait until he (the troublesome patient) messes around with Mr. So-and-So (a potentially assaultive patient); he'll take care of him". By relaxing vigilance and permitting one patient to assault another in a case
such as this, the aide not only achieves some satisfaction of
his aggressive feelings toward the patient but also uses the
incident to demonstrate to the doctor or nurse the need for
better management of the patient.

Many strains are apparent in settings in which the myth
of the dangerous patient is exploited by nursing personnel to
vent their anger and gain prestige. In the light of the foregoing discussion, techniques such as those employed by the
new ward doctor in this case are questionable. He attempted
to teach the aides a lesson only to have them retaliate in kind.

60

CASE 11. *Multiple Seduction*

Mr. S, a 19-year-old veteran of two reformatories and the state penitentiary, was admitted to the hospital by a court order following the attempted rape of a 43-year-old woman on the day that he had been paroled from prison. He was of dull normal intelligence, small in stature, and unattractive. However, he was friendly, courteous, and extremely attentive to the student nurses on the ward, one of whom, Miss A, became quite involved with him. She talked at length with the resident psychiatrist about this patient. The doctor, young and inexperienced, did not report any of these discussions to the head nurse; instead, he focused on the more lurid aspects of the patient's previous sexual behavior. The doctor and this student nurse began dating regularly. These unusual circumstances provided the setting for the following disruptive entanglement.

The patient was interviewed and presented to the class of affiliate students (including Miss A) as an example of a manipulative, sociopathic individual. One week later, following lunch, Mr. S eloped. Soon after, Miss A sought out the housemother to state her fear that the patient would try to see her at the nurses' residence. When questioned, she admitted having given the patient the telephone number and address of one of her relatives with whom she visited on weekends. Further questioning brought out that she felt sorry for the patient, considered him a victim of circumstances, did not feel that he was in any way mentally ill, and was convinced that the ward personnel (with the exception of the resident) mistreated him. The housemother told the student to discuss her feelings about the patient with her instructor. Miss A agreed but did not do this.

A few hours later the patient was returned to the hospital. The next morning he again eloped, and a few minutes after leaving the ward he was seen on the grounds talking to Miss A. She did not report his elopement to anyone, but some of the other students who had seen the patient talking to her told the housemother, who then reported this to the instructor. When questioned, Miss A freely, almost defiantly, admitted that she had not intended to report the patient because "he is such a sweet person and I wanted him to have a chance to go out and get a job and make something of himself". Several nights later when she and two other student nurses were together in an apartment in town, Mr. S telephoned and asked her to meet him in a downtown bar. Miss A became very frightened and notified the hospital authorities.

Later, apprehended and in jail, Mr. S made a number of accusations against Miss A, in regard to her dating the resident.

Mr. S was unusually skilled in making others feel sorry for him. In addition to obtaining sympathy, his ability to involve the nurse in conversations with sexual overtones served to reassure him that he was sexually attractive to women, and gave him stature with other patients in his age group. Always in the background was his need to flout and subvert authority.

Miss A's needs included elements of adolescent rebellion against authority; she had had minor disciplinary problems in the past.

She was not the sort of nurse who is vulnerable because of strong needs to "mother" patients. She had been influenced by her over-identification with the patient as an underdog who was misunderstood, and by the direct excitement of their discussion on sexual matters. The resident psychiatrist abetted the acting out. He had actually encouraged interest in the patient's sensational sexual escapades. In addition, his participation facilitated Miss A's flimsy rationalizations about her interest in the patient.

The needs of the resident are relevant to a more complete understanding. He was also being seductive with the student in his conversations about the patient. First, his talks with her were almost exclusively concerned with the patient's seductive behavior toward her; little was said about the management of the patient. Second, he did not report any of this to the nurse in charge of the students, which indicates some guilt on his part arising from the unprofessional elements in his own behavior. Third, he began dating the nurse at this time and joined her with other students and their dates on weekend parties. The resident, as an active participant in the process, needed to prevent the student from seeing the patient as being mentally ill. He used his discussions of the patient's behavior as a part of his own seductive approach to Miss A. It was then necessary to deal with his own guilt. One way to accomplish this was by regarding the patient as not being mentally ill. Since the patient did not exhibit any of the more noticeable symptoms of neurosis or psychosis and had been diagnosed as a sociopathic personality, "depatientizing" him was facilitated.

However, if the doctor presented the patient's behavior to the student as being that of a *psychopath,* with the moral connotations which are inevitably attached, he would seemingly put himself in the position of disapproving seductive behavior. Therefore, to avoid such sabotage of his own designs, he glossed over the sociopathic aspects of the patient's personality and presented him as deprived and misunderstood. By all of these maneuvers the resident also succeeded in denying his own problems. The student's needs made her more receptive to this view and the stage was set for multiple seduction, although it was no longer clear just who was seducing whom.

CASE 12. *Group Check on Reality*

This case involves two female schizophrenic patients, both physically robust women, both on the same ward and, at the time of this occurrence, both nearly symptom-free. Both had grounds privileges and both attended social functions in the hospital.

At one of these functions they met a male patient, a markedly narcissistic psychopathic epileptic individual. This man was notorious for his flirtations with female patients. During the dance he approached the two women and intense two-person relationships rapidly developed between him and each of the females. Prior to this, the two women had been friendly on the ward. With the advent of the male patient their friendship ceased, they stopped talking, avoided each other, and there was a recurrence of persecutory ideas. The nurses became anxious and frightened, expecting a fight and other unspecified unpleasant happenings to occur.

On the initiative of a head nurse, the ward administrator arranged a meeting with the two female patients and a number of others with whom the man had had similar previous intense relationships. The senior nurse explained to all the patients at the meeting that two patients in the group were at odds over this man, and asked for their comments. The nurse's statement was immediately followed by roars of laughter from all the uninvolved patients who immediately proceeded to tell of their experiences with this man, telling how he had promised to marry them, how he would help them to obtain and pay for divorces, although he, in fact, had no money and used females only for his own gratification. In the face of this new information the two patients started to relax and began to ask questions. Initially, each insisted that the man was serious in his attentions. Gradually, under

pressure of evidence given by other patients, they started
doubting and cross-checking with each other. Lastly, both
turned on the nurse. Why hadn't she warned them? The nurse
apologized and stated that it was too late for warning by the
time the situation was recognized. Why didn't the hospital
protect patients from such happenings? The nurse pointed
out that the man was ill and that when his privileges were
refused, as they had been in the past, he became much worse.

Following this discussion which lasted over an hour, the
two patients re-established their positive relationship with
each other and the over-all tension on the ward rapidly
diminished.

CASE 13.   *Vulnerability to Patient's Perceptiveness*

Mr. P. was a financially successful, 53 year-old real estate
broker who was admitted to the hospital following a two-week
period of hyperactivity, during which he had slept very little,
ceased to be concerned with his personal appearance, and displayed increasingly poor judgment in his business dealings.

On admission he attempted to assume control over the
situation with considerable urgency and to make it clear to
the nurse that he was not to be reduced to patient status.
His first remark was, "I'm very interested in seeing firsthand
just what you do for these people here". He then continued
at length, in a confidential and convincing way, to inform
the nurse that he played a prominent part in the activities
of the local mental health association, and was on intimate
terms with several of the hospital officials.

Contrary to the usual admission procedure, the nurse first
offered to show him around the ward. Mr. P readily agreed,
and by his interested, intelligent questions and his authoritative bearing soon took command of the tour, placing the nurse

in the role of guide. Within twenty minutes, he had inspected the entire ward, with special attention to the kitchen and bathrooms, had introduced himself to the majority of patients and staff, and had demonstrated how the number of chairs in the day room (with adequate reading light) could be doubled by rearranging three lamps. His speech became rapid, his body movements were accelerated, and his authoritative but polite requests became demands.

In an attempt to regain control of the situation which she now realized was out of hand, the nurse abruptly said, "You have seen enough of the ward. Come with me, and we will complete your admission. You must take a shower. I'll take your clothes and have them marked." The patient replied in a loud voice, "Young lady, you will not take my clothes, and I do not need a shower. I've got a hell of a lot to do and, from the looks of this place, so have you. Now, I'll just move one of these tables out in the hall for a desk, and I'll need that pen and paper you have there."

The patient reached out and took the pen from the nurse's pocket and jerked the clipboard of admission forms from her hand. The nurse made no effort to prevent his taking these things and, without a word, turned and rapidly walked into the nurse's station. She immediately called three male aides, informed them that the patient was excited, and that they were to complete the admission procedure. She then added, "You may have to restrain him to give him his bath. In the meanwhile, I'll call the doctor and get a seclusion order."

The nurse immediately called the resident and told him she felt the patient was becoming "just too manicky". The resident attempted to reassure her, saying he had seen the patient forty-five minutes before, and while he might be a little hyperactive, he would rapidly adjust to the ward. He agreed, however, to see the patient.

When the resident arrived, the patient went to greet him,

shook hands, and said, "Doctor, you were certainly right when you told me that we've got a long way to go on this mental health business. I've got to have more cooperation. . . ."

The doctor interjected, "Mr. P, you *must* complete the admission routine, and then I'll talk to you in my office."

The patient turned to the resident, pointedly looking at a prominent silver capped tooth about which the doctor was unduly sensitive, and said: "All that glitters is not gold; you must be a sterling character, and I'd like to see you in *my* office".

The resident replied, "Mr. P, I'll see you only after you've done what the nurse has asked you to". He then walked into the nursing station, wrote the seclusion order, and instructed the aides to complete the admission of the patient.

The provocative behavior of the patient (his grabbing the nurse's pen and papers, etc.) does not appear to be commensurate with such an intense flight and fright reaction from the nurse—especially when this particular nurse had had considerable experience with disturbed patients. A closer look at the data, however, shows several additional sources of apprehension, some or all of which could have produced this reaction. First, the patient was successful in insidiously gaining control and completely dominating the situation. He accomplished this by capitalizing on his accurate perception of the nurse's need to accede to those in authority as well as her concern with social status. The nurse, in turn, perhaps due to these same needs, focused on the healthy, well-organized aspects of the patient's behavior, ignoring the pathological implications. Thus, the nurse relinquished her authority and thereby impaired her ability to structure the situation necessary for the patient's treatment.

The nurse, instead of protecting the patient by restricting the amount of stimulation, actually exposed him to excessive stimuli by taking him on a complete tour of the ward. By the time she perceived the patient's hyperactivity, she could no longer smoothly effect control over the patient's behavior. The patient's complete rejection of her crude and desperate attempts to set limits served to further increase her apprehension; as a result, when he jerked the pen and paper away from her she reacted as if she had been subjected to actual physical assault.

The doctor was also vulnerable to the patient's aggressive perceptiveness. The patient's cutting reference to his silver tooth and "sterling character" struck the resident, and he responded by withdrawing from the patient. By writing the seclusion order, he re-enforced the nurse's inaccurate assessment of the patient's behavior. This nurse had in the past been quite successful in caring for overactive patients. It might be helpful to view her inadequacy in the present instance.

Frequently, in nursing texts, behavioral hyperactivity is considered as an entity, and principles and procedures for patient-care do not take into consideration essential qualitative differences in hyperactivity. Excited behavior of a random, non-goal-directed type such as is often seen in schizophrenia elicits different emotional responses on the part of the nurse than the more goal-directed, more controlling behavior of the manic patient. Behavior of the latter kind, with direction and purposefulness, often arouses much more anxiety in the staff than an equal degree of disorganized hyperactivity. One explanation of this reaction lies in the fact that the diffuse non-purposeful type of over-activity is sufficiently alien to the nurse's own feelings so that there is little possibility of her identifying with this aspect of the patient. On the other hand, as in the incident above, the purposefulness and goal-directedness of the patient's over-active behavior sufficiently corresponded to similar feelings within the nurse so that some identification was possible, and control over her own impulses was threatened.

CASE 14.   *Conflicting Therapeutic Goals—*
           "Furor Therapeuticus"

Mr. J, a 38-year-old lawyer, was admitted to the hospital
because of increasing signs of depression, characterized by
feelings of hopelessness, self-deprecation, anorexia, and in-
somnia. One year prior to the current admission Mr. J had
been hospitalized with approximately the same symptoms. At
the time of the earlier admission, a series of disturbing external events (including severe illnesses of three members of
his family and the birth of his first child) seemed to precipi-
tate the depressive reaction. During the first admission, the
patient was treated by six electroconvulsive treatments and
was discharged in a somewhat improved state. Subsequently,
however, his condition deteriorated and he was referred to a
psychoanalyst who worked with him psychotherapeutically.
Nevertheless, the depressive symptoms recurred, necessitat-
ing the second admission.

The therapist treating him in the hospital decided to institute a course of "regressive" therapy. Being aware that this
form of treatment was not commonly carried out in this particular hospital, the psychiatrist recognized the necessity for
communication with nursing personnel regarding his plan of
treatment. On the day of admission he wrote the following
note on the patient's chart:

> This patient is to be on a program of encouraging regres-
> sion. He has consented to this plan, but is very frightened
> of his deep wishes to regress which he has to deny. There-
> fore, I think that the best plan to follow is to accept any
> tendencies and movements to regression—e.g., sleeping late,
> not shaving, meals in bed, etc.—but not to push him. He
> should proceed at his own pace and at his own time. Pay
> particular attention to bodily needs and wants. Milk and
> food-ad-lib, hot water bottles, massage, etc. should be freely
> given when he asks, but do not push these. It is not neces-
> sary to try to engage him in conversation or try to get him

interested in things. If he initiates conversation, by all means
respond, but keep to the topics he brings up. Specifically,
do not talk about his work (law) or his family. If he seems
to withdraw, there is no need to intervene, just note in the
nurses' notes.

During the following months, problems developed in the
application of the treatment plan at various phases of hospitalization. The head nurse, especially, had a great deal of
difficulty in carrying out the treatment program. Mr. J's admission coincided with an energetic attempt to develop an
integrated program of recreational, occupational, and group
therapeutic activity on this particular nursing unit. Frequent
patient group meetings were being held. Some of these were
decision-making groups; others involved group psychotherapy. Morale was quite high, and an implicit attitude of "we
can help these patients to get well quickly" permeated the
air. However, for most of the personnel this meant that all
patients ought to participate in the group activities. Consequently, the head nurse, who played an important part in
coordinating the *milieu* program, found it difficult to see why
Mr. J should not participate. She encouraged his attendance
at the group meetings and recreational activities by simply
notifying him of their occurrence. A large number of student
nurses were also working on this section and frequently con-
tacted Mr. J in a manner similar to that of the head nurse.
With the backing of personnel, patients also played a role
in putting pressure on Mr. J to be active.

One complicating factor which made it very difficult for
the nurses to support the treatment plan was that they were
supposed to watch for cues from Mr. J rather than to encour-
age regression. In other words, they were told to interact
with him sufficiently to be able to support his wish to stay in
bed, to be fed, and follow his spontaneous desires. The head
nurse found herself very uncomfortable in this type of interaction, and it was impossible for her to desist from giving

him verbal as well as non-verbal cues designed to facilitate his being a group member. Although the therapist was a highly respected and well-liked person, resentment developed in the head nurse and in other personnel as the treatment plan unfolded.

Despite these problems, the patient gradually deepened his regressive activity. At his own request, he was moved to a private room, remained in bed most of the day, kept his blinds down, and occasionally asked for extra food. As this type of behavior developed, the earlier problem became even more explicit, and the head nurse commented on the chart and also informally, saying, "We really aren't doing anything for this man. I don't think that this type of program can succeed". Staff meetings brought out strong differences of opinions, especially between the head nurse and a staff nurse (Nurse F) who was comfortable in carrying out the prescribed plan. The treatment finally reached a crisis phase when the dissension was at its maximum. On two occasions, meals were not brought into the patient's room, and he became panicky with fear of abandonment. At this point the therapist wrote the following:

> The patient has now come to the point of regressing to the extent of staying in bed most of the day. This regression must be supported in a practical way if he is to benefit from it. The patient fears that he will be abandoned, especially at mealtime. This must not happen. Someone must take the responsibility of seeing that Mr. J is fed. There have been two lapses in this connection to date and the patient has used this to justify his fears of abandonment. If the proper connectional experience, i.e., being looked after if he asks for it, is not given to him, there is no point to his being in the hospital and regressing. Personnel, as far as possible, should be available to him if he wants to talk, wants food, milk, warmth, blankets, etc. Do not push patient but continue to be available to look after his needs if he requires it. If the patient stays in bed all day, someone should drop in at least once an hour to see if he wants anything.

71

Finally, the staff resolved the crisis by asking Nurse F to pay closer attention to Mr. J since she seemed to have maintained a good relationship with him and was in agreement with the treatment plan. As might be expected, however, there was some difficulty when the head nurse (who continued to harbor latent doubts about the treatment plan) expressed concern that Nurse F was devoting too much of her time to this patient, to the detriment of the rest of the group. Eventually a compromise was worked out in which Nurse F took responsibility for the patient but was supported in this by two student nurses assigned to the patient.

After about eight months in the hospital, the patient spontaneously expressed a desire to "do more," after what the therapist called "the nadir of the regression." Shortly after this, he was able to leave the hospital and, on a three-year follow-up, has done well. It is interesting that two years later, while still in psychotherapy, he recalled his feelings at the point of emergence from the "nadir" by saying that at that point he had almost become incontinent and that was too shameful for him.

Mr. J's course in the hospital was complicated by two major problems in the nursing personnel. During the first phase of hospitalization, the problem was characterized by the staff's therapeutic ambition which was in conflict with the prescribed treatment. During the latter phase, the problem was characterized by a punitive response on the part of several nurses to the patient's wish for punishment.

Therapeutic Ambition
In Conflict with Prescribed Treatment

This problem was best illustrated by the reaction of the head nurse to the prescribed *regressive* therapy, which seemed to contradict her notion that all patients should get better fast. Part of her problem was related to the therapeutic ambition of the psychiatrist administrator on that nursing unit. Together, they had developed a plan designed to reintegrate seriously ill patients rapidly. It had proven effective in treating many acutely psychotic individuals, as judged by rapid readjustment and return to the community of a significant number of patients.

Underlying problems in the head nurse, however, played a decisive role in her opposition to the prescribed treatment for Mr. J. She unconsciously envied the patient and wished that she, too, could have a "vacation" from adult responsibility. She was threatened by this envy and fearful that she could not control it. Consequently, her motives in subtly encouraging his participation in group activity largely represented a way of solving her own reaction to "regressive" therapy. Since many other members of the personnel shared in her particular problem, it was easy to get mutual support, albeit phrased in rationalizations. Nurse F did not have this conflict and she was able to function quite effectively with Mr. J.

Punitive Responses
To Patient's Wish for Punishment

The patient entered the hospital with a strong need to be punished for his *childish* behavior. His masochistic orientation invited punishment, and it soon was forthcoming. To a certain extent, the encouragement for his participation in ward activities was a type of punishment, implying that he was a bad boy if he remained in bed and gratified himself. On the other hand, several actually encouraged him to regress, and this was also a form of punishment. The most clear-cut punitive response was seen at the maximal point of

regression when meals were not brought to his room. It was
as if the patient had provoked the nursing personnel into
recreating his earliest traumatic experiences, and they almost
reinforced his psychopathology instead of providing a corrective experience. Fortunately, the staff was able to overcome
the problem and did provide effective care. This was largely
due to the joint efforts of Nurse F along with other members of the personnel and abetted by the patience and per-
sistence of the therapist.

CASE 15.   *Frustration by Negative Response*

During her first week of hospitalization, Mrs. O struggled
against an underlying depressive reaction. She manifested
symptomatology and behaved in a manner ostensibly designed to put some distance between herself and personnel.
She protested that she really did not need to be in the hospital and was not "crazy like the other patients". After a short
period in the hospital, however, Mrs. O's protests became
less vehement, and she began to make tentative approaches
to other patients and personnel.

When Nurse P spent one morning in shampooing and setting several patients' hair, she noticed that Mrs. O was ob-
serving her quite closely and was lingering near the doorway.
It was apparent that the patient's hair needed to be sham-
pooed, and the nurse assumed that the patient's behavior
indicated a desire for a shampoo. When Nurse P completed
her work on another patient, she walked over to the doorway
and asked Mrs. O if she would like to have her hair set.
Somehow frightened by this interaction, Mrs. O responded,
"I am quite capable of doing my hair and I don't need you".
Although taken aback by this response, Nurse P asked the
patient if she had ever thought of cutting her hair shorter to

bring out the natural wave. Mrs. O snapped, "Why should I look like the rest of the patients on this ward with their chopped-off hair? If I want it cut, I'll have it done." She then stormed down the hall back towards her room.

Nurse P stood in the doorway, feeling useless, helpless, and irritated by the turn of events. She was afraid to approach the patient on this subject again, deciding that it would not be of any use.

Nurse P enjoyed "doing something" for patients whom she felt were helpless. She derived a great deal of satisfaction from being looked upon as a "helpful nurse" and was easily frustrated when patients resisted her efforts. She had a strong wish to be needed and consequently placed herself in situations where she could advise patients and even other members of the personnel who needed assistance. Dependent patients who reached out for contact and pleaded for help in a direct way were a source of gratification to her. When Nurse P noticed that Mrs. O needed a shampoo, and was standing near the doorway, she correctly interpreted this behavior as a desire on the part of Mrs. O to have a shampoo and she fully expected a positive reaction to her question. When the patient responded in the manner described above, the nurse was offended and felt rejected by the patient. She interpreted the ·response as a personal insult and failed to understand the patient's fear about being hurt in a relationship in which she allowed her dependency feelings to emerge.

Had the nurse not experienced the interaction as a personal injury, she would have been able to explore alternatives to find an area where it was possible to provide therapeutic contact for this patient. It is also quite likely that Mrs. O perceived the nurse's offer for a shampoo as something other than an attempt to make a therapeutic relationship and could not allow herself to accept the offer under

such circumstances. She was frightened that she might somehow be exploited by Nurse P.

CASE 16.   *Nurse Slaps Patient*

A young male patient, Tom, persistently followed the
student, Miss M, around the ward. Each time she turned
around, there was Tom. He would grab her and make sexual advances. She would blush, ask him to "stop" and then
retreat to the nurses' station. When she came out, the same
behavior reoccurred. She tried to talk with him, but he would
constantly interrupt with verbal and physical advances. The
student was too uncomfortable to report this problem. Finally, she gathered "enough courage" to discuss the problem
with the head nurse, who suggested that if it happened again,
"do whatever you would do on the outside". When she returned to the day room, Tom grabbed her again. This time
she slapped his face. She was now angry. Tom was quite surprised and sat down in a chair. Miss M went into the office
to report herself, fearful of what might happen, but was
amazed when the doctor and the head nurse talked the problem through with her and did not "just reprimand her".

Tom, a young, handsome boy, delighted in embarrassing
the young nurses. Originally flattered by his attention, Miss
M soon became uncomfortable, guilty, and angry. She believed that she should not hurt his feelings because he was
a patient. She knew she should treat him in a therapeutic
manner but didn't know how. The doctor explained to Miss
M that Tom was probably taking advantage of her feelings
of inadequacy. He suggested that what she did should be in
line with what she said and felt. This admonition was cor-
rect enough but difficult for her to carry out in view of her
inexperience.

The fact that the head nurse had directed the student to respond to the patient as she would ordinarily respond in a comparable social situation increased the student's difficulty. The head nurse had not taken into account the girl's lack of experience in this kind of situation and thereby failed to give her appropriate support and direction.

The patient, Tom, had sought Miss M out because of her inexperience and vulnerability rather than selecting a more sophisticated person. In a discussion between the doctor, the student, and the head nurse the problem was clarified. Miss M was able to see the results when she demonstrated and felt anger at the same time. She learned that she could have handled the situation appropriately without slapping the patient.

CASE 17. *Nurse-Patient Problems*
Related to Class and Status Differences

Bill was a 13-year-old boy who could best be described as catatonic. He was persistently stiff, rigid, and posturing. He had difficulty coming through the doorway of his room. His expression communicated the hostility underlying the catatonic-like behavior.

He was really a "Little Lord Fauntleroy". He dressed immaculately at all times, expending much of his energy on maintaining an immaculate appearance, and becoming disturbed to the point of tears whenever a smudge appeared on his hands. In this context it is important to note that the patient came from an old New England family that had always emphasized fine manners and proper behavior.

Miss C, a nurse with five years of psychiatric experience, felt that the boy needed to engage in work and play and scuffling, and get his hands dirty as was common in her experience with other boys his age. The patient's doctor went along with Nurse C's attitude, since he knew that she was particularly effective in working with patients of this age. He felt that a lot could be left up to her own feeling and judgment in this situation. He noticed, however, that the boy often felt more comfortable when he was in the company of one of the older male attendants who treated him in a gentle fashion and acted as a friendly older companion.

The physician was very frequently consulted by the patient's mother. The mother was a very anxious, compulsive person, apparently highly disturbed about the patient's illness.

On several occasions when the patient was beginning to relax and get more comfortable he froze into states of immobility which lasted for days when he saw his hands were dirty and his suit rumpled after he had engaged in work or play with Miss C.

A staff conference brought out the point that the patient's whole pattern of daintiness was directly reinforced by his upbringing and cultural background. His training from his mother and father had been in this direction. He had been attending a "very proper" boys' school, at which the pupils were expected to maintain an immaculate appearance. The onset of this illness occurred in another school which was much more liberal and democratic and encouraged the boys to dress in a more informal way.

It became apparent that Miss C had little acceptance of the patient's cultural background. Her own ethnic and cultural background of a working family, half Irish and half Italian, with a somewhat tomboyish youth, gave her an acceptance of the more everyday work and play needs of younger patients but very little acquaintance with the depth of indoctrination in propriety that the patient had received.

Although the nurse could intellectually appreciate that

she had pushed the boy in a direction that was painful to him, she believed that she had been therapeutic in her work with him. It was difficult for her to understand patients whose life experiences, class, and status 'were so utterly different from her own.

The doctor had based his acceptance of the nurse's work with the patient on the generalization that this nurse worked with younger patients, but he hadn't seen clearly the potential conflict between the norms of the nurse and the patient.

CASE 18. *Conflict Between Professional and Personal Moral Standards*

The young, very proper student walked into the day room. Stretched out on a sofa was a young male patient, openly masturbating. The student turned, walked out of the day room, and encountered a male nurse entering the day room. He asked her what was wrong as her facial expression indicated that she was upset. She said, "That nasty Mr. X is at it again, and I wish you would do something about his acting like that in the day room". The student nurse went into the office and asked the head nurse why such activity was allowed. She further stated that Mr. X should be put in his room. The entire response was inconsistent with her previous relationship with this patient.

In this situation, the student was repulsed by Mr. X's behavior. She was rejecting him as well as his activity. She had many feelings about "such things" and could not in any way accept this as part of the patient's illness. She could see that the patient was withdrawn, that he responded to voices, that he had to be encouraged in everything that he did in regard to his appearance—this was part of his illness. This she accepted, but masturbation was something else. The

79

student had definite ideas of "right" and "wrong," and was very much concerned about moral standards. As long as the patient did whatever she thought was morally "right" she accepted him; when he did something she considered "wrong" she rejected him completely. To disapprove of the behavior and direct the patient to other types of activity was at that time out of the question because she also disapproved of the patient. Here the student was not able to use herself therapeutically because her feelings got in her way. Her own concept of "wrong behavior" resulted in her rejecting everything about the patient and left no opportunity for her to help him.

The student's conflict was in having to deal therapeutically with the patient's needs and limitations, as an expression of a whole person, while at the same time experiencing in herself considerable disapproval of the specific disturbing behavior. This nurse had previously expressed her feelings to the instructor that anything remotely concerned with sex was bad and she couldn't talk about it. In her own background, "things pertaining to sex" were not proper and they were not discussed. Therefore, she had a great deal of difficulty with problems of this type.

The nurse's reaction was not entirely inappropriate, except that she confused her feeling about sexual behavior with her judgment about the patient. The area of her problem is indicated by the fact that she was able to accept all of the psychotic activity as an indication of illness, at the same time that she rejected the patient completely because of his open masturbation. This was hinted at in the initial description of this nurse as a young and *proper* student. The inconsistency in her response to difficult aspects of the patient's behavior should be the focal point of discussion in individual supervision.

CASE 19. *Displacement of Conflict with*
Senior Family Members to Geriatric Patient

Mrs. B was an 80-year-old patient with an agitated, senile psychosis who constantly talked about her daughter as if she were her mother. She pleaded to be taken home to her "mother," asking almost continually when somebody would come for her.

Most of the personnel found her quite easy to get along with and believed that she was a sweet and cooperative person albeit confused. She smiled very pleasantly whenever she was given special attention.

Nurse D, a psychiatric nurse with four years' experience at a large state hospital and a private mental hospital, was often the head nurse responsible for her care, and gave her quite a bit of special attention. She appeared to have a very real understanding of this older patient's needs and seemed to be meeting them.

However, Nurse D experienced a number of problems with the patient's daughter, Mrs. C, who could not relinquish Mrs. B to the care of another. She hovered over her mother and watched her every breath wondering if it would be the last. In addition, she alternated between praising the nurse for her devotion to her mother and blaming her for the slightest deviation of attention to other patients. Much of the pressure from the patient's daughter became focused upon Miss D who maintained the appearance of giving excellent nursing care in spite of this pressure.

No improvement occurred in the patient's agitated demanding behavior; in fact, her demands seemed to increase week by week. The daughter, likewise, became more critical as time passed.

In attempting to determine the reasons for lack of improvement in the patient's behavior in the face of what ap-

81

peared to be excellent nursing care, it was learned that Miss
D was ambivalent about this patient. If one heard her in her
off-duty hours, it was apparent that what she was doing was
a considerable strain and burden to her, and that the strain
was mounting.

The nurse was caught up in a conflict situation similar
to that of the patient's daughter; she shared much of the
feeling of hostility that the daughter demonstrated, together
with a sense of being forced into a compensating attentive-
ness. The intensity of the problem was also related to the
daughter's frequent criticisms of Miss D.

Exploring the background of the nurse's attitude, it was
seen that she had had a difficult time with her own grand-
parents and felt that she had suffered at their hands. One
of the reasons that she had left the private mental hospital
where she had worked previously was that there had been
too many old patients. She had hoped that in this hospital
she would spend more of her time with young schizophrenic
patients with whom she was able to work quite competently.

Looking back over her early weeks with the patient, she
was able to see that she had really over-extended herself,
trying to cover up her distaste for older patients, trying to
be a good nurse in spite of her conflict. This had been misunderstood as real interest by the patient's doctor and the
nursing director, so that she was repeatedly asked to do even
more than she was demanding of herself. It became apparent
later that Miss D was secretly hoping that the patient would
die as she viewed this as the only solution to her dilemma.

It was determined that this nurse could not at this time,
give appropriate nursing attention to older patients without
too much strain on her own resources. Until she resolved
some of the problems connected with her feelings about older
people, she would be unable to give good nursing care to
geriatric patients.

CASE 20. *Conflict Between Therapeutic and Personal Ambition**

Miss Davis, a nurse, met Mrs. Johnson, a psychiatric aide, who had just left the room of Mrs. Calvin, a patient. Mrs. Johnson said that the patient didn't want to be bathed; didn't want to be combed. "I managed," she sighed, "but it isn't one of her good days." Miss Davis became distressed and disappointed by this report. She approached the patient's room with some hesitation, but on entering she behaved toward the patient as if she were unaware of what Mrs. Johnson had told her. Miss Davis said, 'You look pretty today, Mrs. Calvin; your hair is so bright and shiny"—chuckle—"you look just like the weather. It's a bright, shiny, crisp day—the kind that makes a person feel full of pep and makes you want to look through a magazine at the new Fall styles." Miss Davis chattered on cheerfully, even though the patient slid down, drew the covers about her, and closed her eyes. It was as though the patient closed her eyes because she could not bear to watch this previously helpful person be so blind to what was actually going on at the moment. The patient, in effect, receded from what now amounted to an insensitive intrusion by the nurse.

Miss Davis finally noticed the effect that her behavior was having upon Mrs. Calvin. She drew herself up short and thought to herself: "Oh, oh—something is wrong. Why is she pulling away like that? Is it something I've said—something I'm doing. Why do I keep rattling on like this—what's bothering *me*?"

Miss Davis then explored this entire episode with the help of the supervisory nurse. The event was discussed from

*The case is taken from the film *Psychiatric Nursing: Nurse-Patient Relationships,* ANA-NLN Film Service, New York, 1959.

the standpoint of what was interfering with the nurse's therapeutic use of herself. It became clear that the nurse was overly ambitious for therapeutic success with this patient and searched for evidence of improvement or improved personal appearance, interest in the weather and in the current magazines. She focused upon these topics at the price of not noticing the real feelings of the patient and her own intrusion into the situation. The nurse's own need for success was threatened at first by realistic observation of the patient's problems. Her own goals became a barrier to progress. When the nurse acted on the basis of personal overambition to see immediate success instead of meeting the patient's needs, her therapeutic usefulness to the patient was lost or, at best, greatly minimized.

Certainly, every nurse has as her goal the patient's improvement. To implement this goal, however, requires that the nurse observe and assess the patient's behavior in as accurate a way as possible, with a minimal amount of interference from her own problems and inappropriate motivations. In this case, Miss Davis' ambitiousness interfered with her perceptual and observational processes to the detriment of the patient. Fortunately, she was able to realize that something was amiss, located the problem within herself, and sought supervisory help. This type of experience was helpful in her maturation towards becoming a more effective psychiatric nurse.

CASE 21   *Successful Reassessment of a Nursing Plan*

One month after Gretchen, age 19, was separated from her family in order to enter college she began to be troubled by rather profound feelings of inadequacy. She increasingly felt a terrifying sense of strangeness and feared that she was about to be destroyed. Following her admission to the college infirmary, it was immediately apparent that Gretchen was failing to win in her struggle to maintain her usual identity. It became necessary to arrange for further treatment on a psychiatric unit of a general hospital.

Information was obtained from her family that Gretchen had been regarded as a rebellious child, difficult to manage, hard to show affection to, and painfully hesitant in any new situation. On admission to the psychiatric unit Gretchen had a perplexed facial expression. She seemed to want to reach out for something to hold onto but feared what the result might be if she did. She was careless in her grooming, and drooped her head so that her hair covered her face, almost completely hiding her features. She had an offensive body odor and her underclothes were soiled. She threatened her roommate with physical harm and destroyed her roommate's belongings. When the nurses came close to Gretchen she kicked and bit them. Patients became frightened of Gretchen and would leave an area as soon as she entered. During the ensuing weeks of hospitalization Gretchen became more and more resistant to care and was almost completely mute and immobile except for intermittent rages. When approached she resentfully responded with, "I don't care—it makes no difference to me".

The nursing staff initially attempted to solve some of the problems Gretchen presented with a 24-hour "scheduled" nursing care plan which had been effective with other patients. This plan listed everything Gretchen would do on a time schedule. It included suggestions for possible approaches to engage Gretchen's interest in activities, her environment, and personal hygiene. She would be roused out of bed at a definite hour in the morning, bathed and dressed at a particular time, taken to meals, and given some task to com-

plete during the morning period. Her afternoons were
planned similarly and discussed with all the staff who were
concerned with carrying out the plan. It was felt that during
the "thawing out" period of Gretchen's stay on the unit one
could best determine her mood and communicate with her by
taking cues from her changing facial expressions and other
non-verbal signs. Often Gretchen looked angry, paced rest-
lessly, and kicked furniture. Although the nurses tried to be
direct and clear in their approach to Gretchen and in their
expectations of her, she often found ways to end the contacts
with the nurses. It had been hoped that the staff could make
activities and tasks interesting enough for Gretchen so as
to stimulate her to complete them, but she would shortly lose
interest.

Since Gretchen was indecisive, it was often difficult to get
her to commit herself even to a choice of clothing for the day.
When she seemed unable to make such a decision and the
staff would make it for her, Gretchen was resistant. Often
her clothes would become torn in the dressing struggle.

Another problem was the way Gretchen reacted at meal-
time. She would wander in the hallway and peek around the
corner at other patients in the dining room. Sometimes she
abruptly ran from the table, leaving the food untouched. At
other times, she consumed large amounts of food after everyone had left the dining area; but in spite of these brief
periods of gorging herself she lost weight.

There were many angry outbursts from Gretchen in con-
nection with bodily cleanliness. Gretchen would sit rigidly
in the tub while she was bathed, or would struggle to get out
of the tub. Once she told the nurse that she was very modest
and that the staff was intruding upon her need for privacy.
The nurse responded by saying that she respected Gretchen's

feelings about the matter but felt it necessary to help bathe Gretchen until she assumed responsibility for bathing herself. Gretchen screamed out, "Well, get out and let me finish". The nurse left but returned only to find Gretchen sitting defiant and unbathed.

During this phase of treatment, staff morale was at a low ebb because of Gretchen's success at warding everyone off. After a meeting of the entire staff, it was decided that it might be helpful to abandon the "scheduled" nursing care approach and try a less intrusive "one-to-one" way of relating. Only one nurse was assigned on each shift to work with Gretchen, to become acquainted with her needs, but not to expect her to participate in group activities. The remainder of the staff occupied themselves with other patients. In response to this individual approach, the change in Gretchen was dramatic. She started to dress without much assistance and came to meals. She talked more easily and behaved more appropriately with her peers. The next step was to suggest to Gretchen that she move to a room with another student patient. Gretchen agreed, and during a period in which her roommate had a brief but incapacitating physical illness, Gretchen assisted in her care. Shortly thereafter for the first time Gretchen attended a scheduled psychotherapy hour, talked in an appropriate manner with only some slight hesitation, and seemed quite proud of her efforts.

Sometimes it is extremely difficult for a nursing staff to sense with any degree of certainty what a patient feels as he experiences a sudden loss of his identity. Success in *feeling with* the patient is often a crucial determinant as to whether a patient elects to seek new solutions for the problems of living in the present or continues to live as if the present were identical with the distant past. No sooner had

Gretchen separated from her familiar home and environment than she began to be troubled by a sense of terrifying strangeness and was able to employ only the most primitive of emotional reactions in coping with her sudden separation from her family. In the hospital she chose either to fight off what she interpreted as the staff's attempt to punish and destroy her, or to withdraw. Nevertheless, some part of her tried hesitantly to reach out. It was in the setting of her intermittent rages and withdrawals, her inability to assume responsibility, her resistive and negative feelings, that the nurses struggled to provide a sense of consistency and guidance. But in response to almost every move toward Gretchen, she complained that the nurses were intruding. She was furious when the nurses made decisions for her, but petulantly refused to make choices of her own.

Nevertheless, after a period of groping, the nurses devised a means for assisting Gretchen in coming out of her entrenched position. Instead of continuing to make unrewarding group efforts to relate to Gretchen, the staff decided to assign only a very few of its members to care for her—a remedy which better fitted in with Gretchen's needs. When only one nurse at a time approached Gretchen, she was able to reach out and respond appropriately. A two-year-old, for example, is often bewildered by too great expectations from too many persons and is often much more comfortable in testing out, bit by bit, how well he can move toward just one person. Given this opportunity, Gretchen began to show signs of improvement almost immediately. She not only permitted a nurse to be near her but also trusted herself to get close to someone else, in this instance a patient, in the guise of caring for her. It was through this series of events that Gretchen was able to reestablish a sense of her own identity.

CASE 22. *Recognition of Staff Discouragement and Projected Blame*

Maurice, a 24-year-old man, had been hospitalized several years for a schizophrenic reaction, catatonic type. Over the years the severity of the symptoms had varied but in general he had been underactive, relatively unresponsive to questioning, and required help in feeding and dressing himself. Various shock therapies and attempts at psychotherapy had led to transitory improvement but it had never been sustained. A few days after his transfer from a state hospital to a small private psychiatric hospital he became mute, motionless, incontinent, and would not feed himself.

It was decided that the nursing plan should take care of the patient's obvious physical needs and at the same time should be utilized as a way of establishing contact with him. An effort was made to create an atmosphere in which Maurice would feel no pressure and would be assured that his needs would be taken care of. At first it was easy to elicit the interest of the nursing staff because his boyish appearance and helplessness evoked in most people a sympathetic desire to help. He was shaved each day; attention was given to his oral hygiene; he was bathed whenever he soiled himself; and he was tube-fed twice daily. Both men and women participated in this program but most of the nursing care involving close physical contact was assigned to student nurses because it was felt that this might be less threatening than if it was done by male attendants.

From the outset the patient's mother was hypercritical of the ward staff. She lived nearby and made frequent, often unannounced, visits. She herself had been hospitalized for a psychotic reaction and made accusations which suggested that she was actively delusional. Her complaints ranged from statements that the ward staff was not showing sufficient

89

interest in her son and was stealing his clothing, to accusations that the staff systematically beat all patients on the
ward, and so forth. Her more preposterous statements caused
only amusement, but her total impact made the staff feel
so uncomfortable that they asked that a limit be placed
on her visits, and her complaints were generally referred to
the ward administrator. Even so, she continued to be a problem, often visiting in the evening, virtually forcing her way
into the ward, and berating the nursing staff.

After several weeks the nursing program for Maurice
began to break down. Various details of his physical care
were forgotten or neglected. Staff members were quick to
criticize each other; some said that Maurice needed more
sympathetic care, while others argued that he was getting
more than his fair share of the staff's attention. Another patient, Paul, began to show his resentment of Maurice by
teasing him. Invariably Paul seemed to have some request
just at those times when several members of the staff were
occupied with the tube-feeding of Maurice. On one occasion
he spit in Maurice's face and on another threatened to strike
him. As tensions grew, the nursing staff asked that the problem of Paul's threats towards Maurice be discussed at the
weekly ward staff meeting.

At this meeting the problem was stated as, "What can
we do about Paul's attacks on Maurice?" As the discussion
of Paul's antagonism to Maurice progressed, a few staff
members mentioned that they themselves had felt some anger
towards Maurice. It developed that almost all the staff members had experienced such feelings in some degree but had
never openly discussed them because the feelings of anger
toward Maurice had been recognized only vaguely or had
seemed too unreasonable.

Most of the staff members described a typical sequence
of events in their relationship with Maurice. Initially they

had felt attracted to him and had been unusually enthusiastic in their efforts to help him. Their eagerness to help had been accompanied by the hope that he would respond favorably. When this did not occur they began to question their ability and had a tendency to withdraw from Maurice. At this point they often had been particularly troubled by the mother's complaints. Once the sequence of special effort, disappointment, withdrawal, and resentment had been recognized many things were seen in a different light. Various staff tensions and anger toward the mother were considered to be displacements of feelings toward Maurice. It was suggested that Paul's behavior might at least in part have been caused by the unrecognized feelings of anger that the staff had toward Maurice. By the end of the meeting the problem had been reformulated from "What can we do about Paul's attacks on Maurice?" to "What can we do about our own feelings of discouragement and resentment caused by the failure of our best efforts to help Maurice?" No answer was proposed for this question but the general feeling of the group was that the discussion had relieved them of a great burden and things did not look so hopeless.

Later the same evening the patient's mother arrived for one of her surprise visits. As the evening attendant listened to the usual recitation of complaints she noticed that she felt more sympathetic toward the mother because it occurred to her that if the ward staff had felt terribly discouraged, the patient's mother must have felt immeasurably worse. As a consequence, she did not try to get rid of the mother but rather encouraged her to talk. At one point the attendant mentioned that she found it difficult to picture what Maurice must have been like prior to his illness. When the mother asked if it would help if she brought in some photographs and high school year books, the attendant encouraged her to do so.

91

The staff was astonished to see the difference in Maurice's appearance and to learn many new things about him. Knowing that he had been a popular class leader and reading about some of his interests in school seemed to change their concept of him. It occurred to one of the attendants that it might make a difference to Paul if he knew some of these things. The effect was truly remarkable. Not only did he discontinue the teasing but he offered to help in Maurice's care. He often sat with him, read him stories, and sometimes played phonograph records to him. Paul had previously resented Maurice because he felt Maurice's helplessness was just an unfair trick to get the attention of the nursing staff. Knowledge of his background gave Paul some appreciation of how intensely disturbed and frightened Maurice must be.

Neither Maurice's condition nor the problems surrounding his care were dramatically changed. His care was still quite taxing to the staff; patients and staff were still, at times, annoyed by the burden. His mother continued to have many criticisms. Nevertheless a crucial step had been made in his treatment. Having recognized and accepted many of their feelings about the patient, the staff did not have to be so defensive. Rather than dissipating their energies in conflict among themselves they could direct their attention to the patient and carry out a basically sound plan of nursing care.

GUIDE FOR USING CLINICAL CASE STUDIES

(PART THREE)

GUIDE FOR USING CLINICAL CASE STUDIES

Barbara B. Buchanan, R.N.*
Helen K. Sainato, R.N.*

VII. INTRODUCTION

The supervisory process is a widely accepted method of teaching psychiatric nursing. Clinical experiences provide the bases for individual or group discussion and subsequent supervision. Care must be exercised to focus on the behavior dynamics of the nurse-patient interaction rather than solely attempting to "analyze the nurse." Too often the instructor permits the supervisory process to turn into a therapy session and all is lost, including the prospective nursing member. This process is threatening to the learner, and for the most part, the instructor is not sufficiently prepared to conduct such sessions. The supervisory process does not involve examination of or probing into the learner's own personal problems but may legitimately involve the nurse's unconscious motivations insofar as they are relevant to the therapeutic qualities of the nurse-patient interaction. Self-examination in the service of improved patient care must remain goal-oriented and consequently circumscribed. As the nurse

* Mrs. Buchanan is Acting Dean of the School of Nursing, University of Miami, Miami, Florida. Mrs. Sainato is Supervisor of Nursing Research at St. Elizabeths Hospital, Washington, D.C.

becomes more skillful in understanding behavior and its significance, she becomes more effective in utilizing inter-personal relationships to help the patient modify his behavior.

Since the advent of the community mental health center and the rising trend toward utilization of the mental health worker (professional and non-professional), large groups of people are now involved in patient care and treatment; this was not true five years ago. There are commonalities in the problems which face staff in dealing with patients and in the planning of their care regardless of the setting—be it hospital or community center. The approach to be utilized in solving these problems depends on the level of worker involved as well as the clinical situation but generally involves group exploration or group techniques. We know of no adequate theoretical model for utilizing group techniques in solving clinical problems.

It is with this background that we have developed an approach for using the clinical examples in Part Two. These examples may be used as a guide for anticipating potential problem areas in patient care. We have found that when TOWARD THERAPEUTIC CARE is used with staff they soon switch from the example which is being discussed in the book to one which is confronting them in their current clinical situation.

Such discussions should include theoretical concepts as a basis for action and prediction rather than relying on "intui-tion." In the clinical cases previously presented, problem areas have been identified to promote discussion which will lead to a better understanding of the nurse's reaction to patient behavior. Questions based on theoretical concepts have been raised.

96

VIII. PROBLEM AREAS

CASE 1. *Withdrawal from the Demanding Patient*

a. Problem Areas

1. Nurse misinterprets patient's bid for closeness and withdraws.
2. Nurse is unable to obtain proper supervision and is immobilized.

b. Questions Based on Theoretical Concepts

1. In terms of the theoretical understanding of paranoid schizophrenia (the patient's illness) did the nurse support the patient's delusion when she used a non-directive approach?
2. From the information presented, what predictions and subsequent intervention could have been made about the nature of the relationship with the female authority figure (counter transference)?
3. The nurse failed to obtain the support and supervision which she needed: What other channels could she have used?

CASE 2. *Meeting the Needs of the Over-Demanding Patient*

a. Problem Areas

1. Whether to meet the needs of patient or staff.
2. Nurse fosters dependency (of patient).
3. Inability to distinguish between depression and acceptable behavior.

b. Questions Based on Theoretical Concepts

1. Consider the variety of responses from staff resulting from the symptoms of dependency as manifested by the patient.
2. The patient is prevented from independent functioning: What are the dynamics of the nurse-patient relationships when this problem is encountered?
3. Instead of "acting out" the patient became reticent and confided her fears to the nurse: Does this change in behavior represent an attempt toward social adjustment?

CASE 3. *Bribery Used for Acceptance*

a. Problem Areas

1. Young nurse's over-identification with patients in her own age group.
2. Inability to accept herself (nurse).

b. Questions Based on Theoretical Concepts

1. The young student was shy, over-compliant, and could not effectively accept or set limits: What prediction and subsequent intervention could have been made concerning the sequence of events which led to the event described?
2. What were the dynamics operating in this illustration (student's over-identification with the teenagers)?

CASE 4. *Honesty vs. Hypocrisy*

a. Problem Areas

1. Staff act human, admit frustration; both staff and patients compromise (solve problem).

2. Staff deny frustration; patients feel "less than human" and act out.

b. Questions Based on Theoretical Concepts

1. The reactions of Ward A staff represents a mature adjustment to frustration: Discuss the importance of the supervisor's role in this situation in meeting the basic security needs of staff.
2. The patients in Ward B were not allowed to make a mature adjustment to the frustrating situation because of the interpersonal techniques which were employed by staff: Discuss the dynamics operating in this situation which resulted in regression and acting out.

CASE 5. *The Professional Person as a Patient*

a. Problem Areas

1. Staff over-identify with patient (graduate nurse) and are unable to accept her as a patient.
2. Staff are intimidated and withdraw supporting behavior.
3. Head nurse indulges her own needs by being the only person who can work effectively with the patient.

b. Questions Based on Theoretical Concepts

1. Identify the patient's underlying problems and needs (not perceived by the staff) which enabled the patient to control her environment.
2. Why did the patient's manipulation evoke the negative responses in staff?
3. Discuss the head nurse's participation in this example (only she could successfully work with the patient): Might this situation meet a basic need for the nurse? Explain.

99

CASE 6. *Placing the Blame*

a. *Problem Areas*

1. Staff were not able to assess the patient's needs and intervene.
2. Staff projected their own feelings of guilt onto administrative changes within the institution.

b. *Questions Based on Theoretical Concepts*

1. The diagnosis of depression and history of suicidal preoccupation were important in this clinical example. Taking this information into account and the orders which were written by the physician, what cues did the staff fail to communicate? What intervention would have been appropriate? What was really going on between the nursing staff and the physician?
2. The patient's need for supervision was identified by the charge nurse, yet no restrictions or limitations were placed on the patient's activity. Discuss these factors in terms of the staff's basic insecurity and subsequent anxiety.

CASE 7. *Blackmail with "Gifts"*

a. *Problem Areas*

1. Staff fail to assess patient's need for acceptance.
2. Staff satisfy their own needs for acceptance and promote manipulative behavior.

b. *Questions Based on Theoretical Concepts*

1. The nursing staff failed to identify the patient's need for acceptance: Describe the situation and

subsequent behavior which should have helped the
staff in providing a more realistic plan of care for
this patient.

2. It is important to have an understanding of the
   ward situation at the time an "incident" occurs:
   Discuss this statement in relation to the Christmas
   season.

CASE 8. *The Patient as a Victim of Misunderstanding
in Supervision*

a. *Problem Areas*

1. Nurse/doctor disagreement over patient management.
2. Nurse is unable to cope with her hostile feelings
   for the doctor and "stretches rules" for the patient.

b. *Questions Based on Theoretical Concepts*

1. The nurse was unable to cope with her hostile feelings about the physician and "stretched the rules"
   for the patient: What dynamics were involved in
   this nurse-patient relationship?
2. The physician and the nurse disagreed about patient management: What other means could the
   nurse have used in solving this problem? What
   conflicts might the nurse be experiencing?

CASE 9. *Contrasting Expectations*

a. *Problem Areas*

1. Nurse intimidates patient and provokes hostility.
2. Nurse reacts to patient's hostility with hostility.

101

b. Questions Based on Theoretical Concepts

1. The nurse felt her professional competence threatened and intimidated the patient who responded with hostility: Discuss the nurse's defensiveness and inability to assess the situation.

2. Do you agree with the statement "the nurse expected trouble and she got it"? Why?

CASE 10. Myth of the "Dangerous Patient" as Exploited by the Ward Personnel

a. Problem Areas

1. Staff perpetuate myth in order to increase their own prestige and status (being able to work on disturbed ward).

2. Staff cover up their own aggressive tendencies and disagreements about patient management and treatment by relaxing vigilance and promoting patient fights.

b. Questions Based on Theoretical Concepts

1. The doctor used the patient to get back at the aides; the nursing staff used the patient to perpetuate the myth of the dangerous patient: Discuss staff motivations in this illustration.

2. Staff reassure themselves of their own self-control by suppressing patient fights; on the other hand, they can relax vigilance and permit one patient to assault another, thereby demonstrating to staff in charge the need for better management of patients: What inner conflicts are staff displaying?

CASE 11. *Multiple Seduction*

a. *Problem Areas*

1. Young staff members' over-identification with patient in their own age group.
2. Failure to communicate information.
3. Inability to accept themselves (student and resident), so they "depatientize" the patient.

b. *Questions Based on Theoretical Concepts*

1. The resident talked to the student about the patient's seductive behavior, did not discuss management of patient, failed to communicate his discussions with the student to the Head Nurse, began dating the student, and regarded the patient as *not* being mentally ill: Discuss the resident's need to "depatientize" the patient.
2. The student over-identified with patient, felt sorry for him, thought he was mistreated, failed to communicate information to the instructor; in short, prevented the patient from being treated as a patient: What are the dynamics of the nurse-patient relationships when this problem is identified? (Consider rebellion against authority.)

CASE 12. *Group Check on Reality*

a. *Problem Areas*

1. Two nearly symptom-free female patients who were good friends were individually wooed by the same male patient.
2. As intense relationships developed between the male patient and each of the females, the women avoided each other and their previous symptoms reappeared.

103

3. The nurses became anxious; a meeting was arranged with the two women and a number of others with whom the man had had similar experiences.

b. *Questions Based on Theoretical Concepts*

1. The nurse arranged a meeting so that the two women involved could confront other patients who had been previously involved with same man: Why did the nurse arrange for this type of confrontation?
2. Could the nurse have been as successful if she had attempted to talk to the patients herself?

CASE 13. *Vulnerability to Patient's Perceptiveness*

a. *Problem Areas*

1. Nurse fails to make proper assessment of patient's behavior and is powerless to structure the situation as patient takes over.
2. Doctor is insulted by the patient, withdraws, and reinforces the nurse's inaccurate assessment of patient.
3. Doctor and nurse over-react and become punitive.

b. *Questions Based on Theoretical Concepts*

1. Compare the hyperactive behavior as exhibited by the patient who is in manic excitement and a patient who is in a catatonic excitement state.
2. Discuss the forms of counter-aggression utilized by staff in response to patient's perceptiveness of staff vulnerability.
3. What are the major needs of this overactive patient? What would be covered by a nursing-care plan to meet these needs including short- and long-term nursing goals?

104

CASE 14. *Conflicting Therapeutic Goals—*
"Furor Therapeuticus"

a. Problem Areas

1. Head nurse's conflict over prescribed management of patient (which was contrary to the ward program), resulting in disregard for patient's program.
2. Differences of opinions regarding patient-staff dissension increased, resulting in punitive treatment.
3. Head nurse solved her problem by assigning patient to staff nurse.

b. Questions Based on Theoretical Concepts

1. In anticipation of problem areas concerning modes of treatment which differ markedly in approach, what are some ways of minimizing staff conflicts?
2. What concepts provide the rationale for treatment of patients with anaclitic depression? When is this mode of treatment contraindicated?
3. Contrast the basic underlying conflicts and use of symptom formations between this depressed patient and one who exhibits the symptoms of a schizophrenic, catatonic state.

CASE 15. *Frustration by Negative Response*

a. Problem Areas

1. The nurse's need to be accepted and useful rendered her helpless when the patient rejected her offer.
2. Nurse failed to understand patient's fear of allowing her dependency feelings to emerge.

b. *Questions Based on Theoretical Concepts*

1. Discuss passivity as a mode of interaction with others.
2. What are some examples of non-intrusive participation exhibited by patients?
3. With what groups of patients can the nurse with the needs illustrated in this example work most effectively?

CASE 16. *Nurse Slaps Patient*

a. *Problem Areas*

1. Student felt inadequate, sought help from head nurse who failed to give her appropriate direction.
2. Student's inability to differentiate between social and professional behavior.

b. *Questions Based on Theoretical Concepts*

1. As the head nurse, how would you supervise the student in this situation to prevent this incident? Describe the supervisory process immediately following the incident.
2. Discuss the implications of social versus professional interaction in a psychiatric setting. Cite examples and illustrate possible outcomes of interactions handled in a professional versus social context.

CASE 17. *Nurse-Patient Problems Related to Class and Status Differences*

a. *Problem Areas*

1. Physician agreed to nurse's plan of care for a teen-

ager because of her previous work with young patients.

2. Nurse could not understand or work successfully with the patient whose norms were different from her own.

b. Questions Based on Theoretical Concepts

1. Discuss the nature of prejudice. Give examples of ways that this affects patient response to staff and staff response to patients.
2. Contrast class and status differences in regard to the male and female role, handling of grief, expressions of anxiety, and attitudes towards authority figures.

CASE 18. *Conflict Between Professional and Personal Moral Standards*

a. Problem Areas

1. Student could not accept behavior or the patient when he violated her personal moral standards.
2. Student's own unresolved feelings about sex interfered with her judgment in caring for the patient.

b. Questions Based on Theoretical Concepts

1. Explore the origin and maintenance of "moral standards"; give other examples of conflict between professional and personal standards in this "moral" area.
2. How might discussion about areas of sexual activity be conducted by staff which would benefit this young nurse?

CASE 19. *Displacement of Conflict with Senior Family Members to a Geriatric Patient*

a. Problem Areas

1. Nurse over-extends herself to both the patient and her daughter in an effort to cover up her negative feelings about geriatric patients.
2. The physician and Director of Nursing misinterpreted the nurse's "over-compensation" as good nursing care and demanded more of her.
3. The nurse identified with the patient's daughter and unconsciously promoted the patient's illness because of her own conflict about older patients.

b. Questions Based on Theoretical Concepts

1. What are the factors which go into forming one's attitudes toward the aging process?
2. Define "reaction formation." What are the strengths and weaknesses of this process for the individual?

CASE 20. *Conflict Between Therapeutic and Personal Ambition*

a. Problem Areas

1. Complete disregard for report that patient wasn't doing well in order to fulfill her own needs.
2. Nurse's goals become barrier to progress and patient withdraws.

b. Questions Based on Theoretical Concepts

1. Define anxiety and contrast this with the definition of fear. What are the physiological signs and be-

havioral expressions of the different phases of anxiety?

2. Describe the effects of anxiety on the perceptual field.

3. Describe possible modes of supervisory intervention when the nurse is unaware that her personal needs and goals are negating the therapeutic process.

CASE 21. *Successful Reassessment of a Nursing Plan*

a. *Problem Areas*

1. Difficulty in selecting an approach to patient care.

2. A scheduled program involved too many people, which further alienated patient from staff.

3. A one-to-one approach worked well, gradually extended to others.

b. *Questions Based on Theoretical Concepts*

1. Contrast several ways of assessing patient's needs and formulating nursing goals upon admission.

2. Discuss the points of background information and behavior upon admission which should have precluded the comprehensive "scheduled" nursing care plan.

3. The one-to-one relationship is successful with certain types of patient behavior. Discuss these situations, and how this approach may be modified when it is not practical in a given situation.

CASE 22. *Recognition of Staff Discouragement and*
          Projected Blame

a. *Problem Areas*

1. Staff disappointment, withdrawal, and resentment
   when patient doesn't improve.
2. Staff displaces their own anger toward patient to
   his mother.
3. Fellow patient misinterprets patient behavior as a
   trick to get attention.

b. *Questions Based on Theoretical Concepts*

1. What are some techniques of intervention which
   may be successful in breaking this kind of cycle
   before it results in the staff's "hopeless feeling"
   about a patient?
2. Define and give other illustrations of displacement.
   Cite clinical examples and how these are manifested
   in patient care.
3. Discuss the implications of (a) communicating
   personal information about one patient to another
   and (b) one patient assuming some responsibility
   for another patient.

110

CONCLUDING COMMENTARY

The goals of therapeutic interaction include the patient's better understanding of his needs, his greater facility in communication, his increased social participation, and his more-constructive methods of attaining personal satisfactions. The therapeutic effectiveness of the nurse is directly related both to her understanding of the patient and his illness and to her awareness of her feelings and the impact of her responses. In the face of anxiety, despair, helplessness, regression, and aggression which are ever present in a psychiatric hospital setting, a nurse needs this understanding in order to enter into effective relationships.

Twenty-two clinical case studies and a Guide have been presented to illustrate, identify, and analyze some of the therapeutic problems that arise in nursing care. These problems involve personnel-patient and intra-staff interactions. There is no easy answer to such problems. The theoretical formulations, the clinical examples, and the Guide which comprise this book are not intended to provide definitive answers to all problems. Rather, they provide a framework for studying and resolving problems commonly met by all involved in patient care.

Within the context of this book, the term "nurse" is manifestly generic. The principles and theses formulated are equally relevant and applicable to attendants, psychiatric aides, occupational therapists, physical therapists, recreational therapists, corrective therapists, vocational counselors, volunteer workers, interns, residents—in short, all who participate in the daily life and activities of the sick person.

Abdellah, F. G.: "Methods of Identifying Covert Aspects of Nursing Problems," *Nursing Research,* 6:4-23, June, 1957.

ACTION FOR MENTAL HEALTH, Final Report of the Joint Commission on Mental Illness and Health, John Wiley & Sons, Inc., New York, 1961.

A.N.A. REGIONAL CLINICAL CONFERENCES, Appleton-Century-Crofts, New York, 1968.

Behymer, A. F.: "Interaction Patterns and Attitudes of Affiliate Students in a Psychiatric Hospital," *Nursing Outlook,* 1:205-207, April, 1953.

Bennett, A. E., and Engle, B.: "Psychiatric Nursing and Occupational Therapy," in E. A. Spiegel, ed.: PROGRESS IN NEUROLOGY AND PSYCHIATRY, Vol. 8, Chapter 35, Grune & Stratton, Inc., New York, 1953. Bettelheim, B.: "On Institutional Group Therapy," *Bulletin of the American Psychoanalytic Association,* 6, May, 1950.

——————— and Sylvester, E.: "Therapeutic Influence of the Group on the Individual," *American Journal of Orthopsychiatry,* 17:684-692, October, 1947.

Black, Sister Kathleen M., R.N., R.S.M.: "An Existential Model for Psychiatric Nursing," *Perspectives in Psychiatric Care,* 6:4, 179-184, 1968.

———————: "Appraising the Psychiatric Patient's Nursing Needs," *American Journal of Nursing,* 52:718-721, June, 1952.

Bodie, Marilyn K., R.N., B.S.N.: "When a Patient Threatens Suicide," *Perspectives in Psychiatric Care,* 6:2, 76-79, 1968.

Boyd, R. W.; Baker, T.; and Greenblatt, M.: "Ward Social Behavior: An Analysis of Patient Interaction at Highest and Lowest Extremes," *Nursing Research,* 3:77-80, October, 1954.

Brown, Esther Lucile, Ph.D.: NEWER DIMENSIONS OF PATIENT CARE, Parts 1, 2, and 3, Russell Sage Foundation, New York, 1965.

Bullard, D. M.: "Problems of Clinical Administration," *Bulletin of the Menninger Clinic,* 16:193-201, November, 1952.

Caudill, W.; Redlich, F. C.; Gilmore, H. R.; and Brody, E. P.: "Social Structure and Interaction Processes on a Psychiatric Ward," *American Journal of Orthopsychiatry*, 22:314-334, April, 1952.

—————— and Stainbrook, E.: "Some Covert Effects of Communication Difficulties in a Psychiatric Hospital," *Psychiatry*, 17:27-40, February, 1954.

Chambers, Carolyn, R.N., M.S.: "Nurse Leadership During Crisis Situations on a Psychiatric Ward," *Perspectives in Psychiatric Care*, 5:1, 29-35, 1967.

Clancy, Kathlyn M., R.N., M.S.: "Concerning Gifts," *Perspectives in Psychiatric Care*, 6:4, 169-175, 1968.

Clemence, Sister Madeleine: "Existentialism: A Philosophy of Commitment," *American Journal of Nursing*, 66:3, 500-505, 1966.

Devereaux, G.: "The Social Structure of the Hospital as a Factor in Total Therapy," *American Journal of Orthopsychiatry*, 19:492-500, July, 1949.

Dixson, Barbara K.: "Intervening When the Patient is Delusional," *Journal of Psychiatric Nursing and Mental Health Services*, 7:1, 25-31, January-February, 1969.

Eddy, Frances L., R.N.; O'Neill, Elaine, R.N.; and Astrachan, Boris M., M.D.: "Group Work on a Long-Term Psychiatric Service," *Perspectives in Psychiatric Care*, 6:1, 9-15, 1968.

Eisenberg, Joann, R.N., M.A. and Abbott, Ruth D., R.N., M.S.: "The Monopolizing Patient in Group Therapy," *Perspectives in Psychiatric Care*, 6:2, 66-69, 1968.

Fagin, Claire M.: "Psychotherapeutic Nursing," *American Journal of Nursing*, 67:2, 298-304, February, 1967.

Fox, D. J., and Diamond, L. K.: "The Identification of Satisfying and Stressful Situations in Basic Programs in Nursing Education: A Progress Report," *Nursing Research*, 8:4-12, Winter, 1959.

Frank, J. D.: "Corrective Emotional Experiences in Group Therapy," *American Journal of Psychiatry*, 8:126-131, August, 1951.

Getty, Cathleen, R.N., M.S., and Shannon, Anna M., R.N., M.S.: "Nurses as Co-therapists in a Family-Therapy Setting," *Perspectives in Psychiatric Care*, 5:1, 36-46, 1967.

Gilmore, H.: "The Psychiatrist's Part in Nursing Education Programs," *Nursing Outlook*, 1:217-219, April, 1953.

113

Goffman, E.: INTERACTION RITUAL, Aldine Publishing Co., Chicago, 1967.

Goldberg, N., and Hyde, R. W.: "Role-Playing in Psychiatric Training," *Journal of Social Psychology*, 39:63-75, February, 1954.

Gorton, J. V., R.N., M.A.: A GUIDE FOR THE EVALUATION OF PSYCHIATRIC NURSING SERVICES, National League for Nursing, New York, 1961.

Green, Hannah: I NEVER PROMISED YOU A ROSE GARDEN, Holt, Rinehart & Winston, Inc., New York, 1964.

Greenblatt, M.; Levinson, D.; and William, R. H.: THE PATIENT AND THE MENTAL HOSPITAL, The Free Press, Glencoe, Ill., 1957.

Greenblatt, M., and Simon, B.: "Summary," in Greenblatt and Simon, eds., REHABILITATION OF THE MENTALLY ILL: SOCIAL AND ECONOMIC ASPECTS, American Association for the Advancement of Science, Washington, D. C. 1959.

——————: York, R. H.; and Brown, E. L.: FROM CUSTODIAL TO THERAPEUTIC PATIENT CARE IN MENTAL HOSPITALS, Russell Sage Foundation, New York, 1955.

Gregg, D. E.: "Anxiety—A Factor in Nursing Care," *American Journal of Nursing*, 52:1363-1365, November, 1952.

——————: "The Psychiatric Nurse's Role," *American Journal of Nursing*, 54:848-851, July, 1954.

Group for the Advancement of Psychiatry: THE PSYCHIATRIC NURSE IN THE MENTAL HOSPITAL, *GAP Report No. 22*, New York, May, 1952.

——————: THERAPEUTIC USE OF THE SELF, *GAP Report No. 33*, New York, June, 1955.

——————. ADMINISTRATION OF THE PUBLIC PSYCHIATRIC HOSPITAL, *GAP Report No. 46*, New York, July, 1960.

Hall, B. H.: "A Colleague Looks at Psychiatric Nursing," *Nursing Outlook*, 2:66-69, February, 1954.

Harris, Faye Gary, R.N., M.A.: "A Psychiatric Nursing Experience with a Troubled Child in the Community," *Perspectives in Psychiatric Care*, 5:2, 92-97, 1967.

Hart, B.; PSYCHOLOGY OF INSANITY, 5th ed., Cambridge University Press, Cambridge, England, 1957.

Holmes, Marguerite J., and Werner, Jean A.: PSYCHIATRIC NURSING IN A THERAPEUTIC COMMUNITY, The Macmillan Co., New York, 1966.

Hyde, R. W.: EXPERIENCING THE PATIENT'S DAY, G. P. Putnam's Sons, New York, 1955.

——————: "Factors in Group Motivation in a Mental Hospital," *Journal of Nervous and Mental Disorders*, 3, March, 1953.

—————— and Kandler, H. M.: "Altruism in Psychiatric Nursing," in P. A. Sorokin, ed.: Forms and Techniques of Altruistic and Spiritual Growth, Chapter 25, pp. 387–399, Beacon Press, Inc., Boston, 1954.

—————— and Scott, B.: "The Occupational Therapy Research Laboratory," *Occupational Therapy and Rehabilitation*, 30, June, 1951.

Jones, M.: THE THERAPEUTIC COMMUNITY, Basic Books, Inc., New York, 1953.

Kaldeck, R.: "Group Psychotherapy by Nurses and Attendants," *Diseases of the Nervous System*, 12:138-142, May, 1951.

Kalkman, M. E.: INTRODUCTION TO PSYCHIATRIC NURSING, 2nd ed., McGraw-Hill Book Co., New York, 1958.

Kandler, H. M.: "Studying a Problem in Psychiatric Nursing," *American Journal of Nursing*, 51:108-111, February, 1951.

——————; Behymer, A. F.; Kegeles, S. S.; and Boyd, R. W.: "A Study of Nurse-Patient Interaction in a Mental Hospital," *American Journal of Nursing*, 52:1100-1103, September, 1952.

—————— and Hyde, R. W.: "Changes in Empathy in Student Nurses During the Psychiatric Affiliation," *Nursing Research*, 2:33-36, June 1953.

Kelly, Holly S., R.N., M.S., and Philbin, M. Kathleen, R.N., B.S.N.: "Sociodrama: An Action-Oriented Laboratory for Teaching Interpersonal Relationship Skills," *Perspectives in Psychiatric Care*, 6:3, 111-115, 1968.

King, Joan M., R.N., D.N.Sc.: "The Initial Interview: Assessment of the Patient and his Difficulties," *Perspectives in Psychiatric Care*, 5:6, 256-261, 1967.

Kline, N. S.: "Characteristics and Screening of Unsatisfactory Psychiatric Attendants and Attendant Applicants," *American Journal of Psychiatry*, 106:573-586, February, 1959.

Kloes, Karen B., R.N., M.S., and Weinberg, Ann, R.N., B.S.: "Counter Transference: A Bilateral Phenomenon in the Learning Model," *Perspectives in Psychiatric Care*, 6:4, 152-162, 1968.

Kneisl, Carol Ren, R.N., M.S.: "Increasing Interpersonal Understanding Through Sociodrama," *Perspectives in Psychiatric Care*, 6:3, 104-109, 1968.

Lentz, E.: "Morale in a Hospital Business Office," *Human Organization*, 9:17-21, 1950.

Lesser, M. S., and Keane, V. R.: NURSE-PATIENT RELATIONSHIPS IN A HOSPITAL MATERNITY SERVICE, C. V. Mosby Co., St. Louis, 1956.

Lewis, G. K.; Holmes, Marguerite J.; and Katz, F. E.: AN APPROACH TO EDUCATION OF PSYCHIATRIC NURSING PERSONNEL, National League for Nursing, New York, 1961.

Matheney, R., and Topalis, M.: PSYCHIATRIC NURSING, 2nd ed., C. V. Mosby Co., St. Louis, 1957.

Mellow, June, R.N., Ed.D.: "The Experiential Order of Nursing Therapy in Acute Schizophrenia," *Perspectives in Psychiatric Care*, 6:6, 249-255, 1968.

——————: "An Exploratory Study of Nursing Therapy with Two Persons with Psychosis," Master's thesis (unpublished), Boston University, 1953.

Mereness, Dorothy A., R.N., Ed.D.: "Family Therapy: An Evolving Role for the Psychiatric Nurse," *Perspectives in Psychiatric Care*, 6:6, 256-263, 1968.

——————: "Problems and Issues in Contemporary Psychiatric Nursing," *Perspectives in Psychiatric Care*, 2, 14-21, 1964.

——————: PSYCHIATRIC NURSING: DEVELOPING PSYCHIATRIC NURSING SKILLS, 1, William C. Brown & Co. Publishers, Dubuque, Iowa, 1966.

——————: PSYCHIATRIC NURSING: UNDERSTANDING THE NURSE'S ROLE IN PSYCHIATRIC PATIENT CARE, 2, William C. Brown & Co. Publishers, Dubuque, Iowa, 1966.

Moore, Judith Ann, R.N., M.S.: "Encountering Hostility During Psychotherapy Sessions," *Perspectives in Psychiatric Care*, 6:2, 58-65, 1968.

Morimoto, F. R.: "Favoritism in Personnel-Patient Interaction," *Nursing Research*, 3:109-112, February, 1955.

―――――: "The Socializing Role of Psychiatric Ward Personnel," *American Journal of Nursing*, 54:53-55, January, 1954.

――――― and Greenblatt, M.: "Personnel Awareness of Patients' Socializing Capacity," *American Journal of Psychiatry*, 110:443-447, December, 1953.

Muller, T. G.: THE NATURE AND DIRECTION OF PSYCHIATRIC NURSING, J. B. Lippincott Co., Philadelphia, 1950.

National League for Nursing: THE EDUCATION OF THE CLINICAL SPECIALIST IN PSYCHIATRIC NURSING, National League for Nursing, New York, 1958.

―――――: PSYCHIATRIC NURSING CONCEPTS AND BASIC NURSING EDUCATION, National League for Nursing, New York, 1960.

―――――: THREE REPORTS OF NURSE-PATIENT INTERACTION IN PSYCHIATRIC NURSING, National League for Nursing, New York, 1960.

Nehren, Jeanette G., R.N., M.S., and Larson, Margaret L., R.N., M.N.: "Supervised Supervision," *Perspectives in Psychiatric Care*, 6:1, 25-27, 1968.

Nielsen, J. C.: REPORT OF SECOND NATIONAL PSYCHIATRIC AIDE PROGRAMS WORKSHOP, National Association for Mental Health, New York, August, 1952.

Norris, Catherine M., R.N., Ed.D.: "Psychiatric Crises," *Perspectives in Psychiatric Care*, 6:1, 20-29, 1967.

Noyes, A., and Kolb, L.: MODERN CLINICAL PSYCHIATRY, 5th ed., W. B. Saunders Co., Philadelphia, 1958.

Parks, Suzanne Lowry, R.N., M.S., "Allowing Physical Distance as a Nursing Approach," *Perspectives in Psychiatric Care*, 4:6, 31-35, 1966.

Pearson, G. H. J., and English, O. S.: THE EMOTIONAL PROBLEMS OF LIVING, W. W. Norton & Co., Inc., New York, 1955.

Peplau, Hildegard E., R.N., Ed.D.: ASPECTS OF PSYCHIATRIC NURS-
ING, SECTION B: THERAPEUTIC CONCEPTS, National League for
Nursing, New York, 1957.

——————: "Interpersonal Techniques: The Crux of Psychiatric
Nursing," *American Journal of Nursing*, 57:6, 50-54, June, 1962.

——————: INTERPERSONAL RELATIONS IN NURSING, G. P. Putnam's Sons, New York, 1952.

——————: "Principles of Psychiatric Nursing," in S. Arieti,
ed., AMERICAN HANDBOOK OF PSYCHIATRY, Vol. 2, Chapter 92,
pp. 1842–1856, Basic Books, Inc., New York, 1959.

——————: "Psychotherapeutic Strategies," *Perspectives in Psychiatric Care*, 6:6, 264-270, 1968.

PSYCHIATRIC NURSING CONCEPTS AND BASIC NURSING EDUCATION.
Proceedings of the Conference at Boulder, Colorado, June 15-18,
1959. National League for Nursing, New York, 1960.

Raymond, Sister Marie, R.N., R.S.M.: "Existentialism and the Psychiatric Nurse," *Perspectives in Psychiatric Care*, 6:4, 185-187,
1968.

Render, H. W., and Weiss, O. M.; NURSE-PATIENT RELATIONSHIPS
IN PSYCHIATRY, 2nd Edition, McGraw-Hill Book Co., New York,
1959.

Report of the Surgeon General's Consultant Group on Nursing.
TOWARD QUALITY IN NURSING NEEDS AND GOALS, Public Health
Service Publication, No. 992, United States Government Printing
Office, Washington, 1963.

Richards, Hilda, R.N., Ed.M.; "The Role of the Nurse in the Therapy
of the Lower Socioeconomic Psychiatric Patient," *Perspectives in
Psychiatric Care*, 5:2, 82-91, 1967.

Risley, Joan, R.N., M.N.: "Nursing Intervention in Depression,"
Perspectives in Psychiatric Care, 5:2, 65-76, 1967.

Robinson, A.: THE PSYCHIATRIC AIDE, 2nd ed., J. B. Lippincott Co.,
Philadelphia, 1958.

Ruesch, J.: THERAPEUTIC COMMUNICATION, W. W. Norton & Co.,
Inc., New York, 1961.

—————— and Kee, W.: NON-VERBAL COMMUNICATION, University
of California Press, Berkeley, 1956.

118

Sabshin, M.: "Nurse-Doctor-Patient Relationships in Psychiatry," *American Journal of Nursing*, 57:188-192, February, 1957.

Schwartz, M. S., and Shockley, E.: THE NURSE AND THE MENTAL PATIENT, Russell Sage Foundation, New York, 1956.

———————— and Stanton, A. H.: "Social Study of Incontinence," *Psychiatry*, 13:399-416, November, 1950.

Schwartz, C. G.; Schwartz, M. S.; and Stanton, A. H.: "A Study of Need-Fulfillment on a Mental Hospital Ward," *Psychiatry*, 14:222-242, May, 1951.

Semrad, E. V.; Menzer, D.; Mann, J.; and Standish, C. T.: "A Study of the Doctor-Patient Relationship in Psychotherapy of Psychotic Patients," *Psychiatry*, 15:377-385, November, 1952.

Simon, B.: "New Trends in Rehabilitation" in J. L. Moreno and J. L. Masserman, eds., PROGRESS IN PSYCHOTHERAPY, Vol. 4, Grune & Stratton, Inc., New York, 1959.

————————: "Psychiatric Rehabilitation," *Journal of American Medical Association*, 171:2098-2101, December, 1959.

————————: "The Role of Rehabilitation in Therapy," in Proceedings of Fifth Annual Psychiatric Institute: Discipline in Modern Psychiatric Treatment, New Jersey Neuropsychiatric Institute, Princeton, September, 1957.

Stanton, A. H., and Schwartz, M. S.: "Observations on Dissociation as Social Participation," *Psychiatry*, 12:399-454, November, 1949.

————————: THE MENTAL HOSPITAL, Basic Books, Inc., New York, 1954.

STATEMENT ON PSYCHIATRIC NURSING PRACTICE, Division on Psychiatric-Mental Health Nursing. American Nurses' Association, New York, 1967.

Szurek, S. A.: "Dynamics of Staff Interaction in Hospital Psychiatric Treatment of Children," *American Journal of Orthopsychiatry*, 17:652-664, 1947.

Tudor, G. E.: "A Sociopsychiatric Nursing Approach to Intervention in a Problem of Mutual Withdrawal on a Mental Hospital Ward," *Psychiatry*, 15:193-217, May, 1952.

Von Mering, O., and King, S. H.: REMOTIVATING THE MENTAL PATIENT, Russell Sage Foundation, New York, 1957.

Whitehorn, J. C.: "Emotional Responsiveness in Clinical Interview," *American Journal of Psychiatry*, 94:311-315, 1937.

Woodward, J.: EMPLOYMENT RELATIONS IN A GROUP OF HOSPITALS, Institute of Hospital Administrators, London, 1950.

World Health Organization, Expert Committee on Psychiatric Nursing: FIRST REPORT, Technical Report Series, No. 105, Columbia University Press, New York, 1956.

Zetzel, E. R.: "The Dynamic Basis of Supervision," *Social Casework*, April, 1953.

Zilboorg, G.: "The Struggle of the Patient Against the Doctor," *Journal of the Michigan State Medical Society*, 52, April, 1953.

STATEMENT OF PURPOSE

THE GROUP FOR THE ADVANCEMENT OF PSYCHIATRY has a membership of approximately 300 psychiatrists, most of whom are organized in the form of a number of working committees. These committees direct their efforts toward the study of various aspects of psychiatry and the application of this knowledge to the fields of mental health and human relations.

Collaboration with specialists in other disciplines has been and is one of GAP's working principles. Since the formation of GAP in 1946 its members have worked closely with such other specialists as anthropologists, biologists, economists, statisticians, educators, lawyers, nurses, psychologists, sociologists, social workers, and experts in mass communication, philosophy, and semantics. GAP envisages a continuing program of work according to the following aims:

1. To collect and appraise significant data in the field of psychiatry, mental health, and human relations;

2. To re-evaluate old concepts and to develop and test new ones;

3. To apply the knowledge thus obtained for the promotion of mental health and good human relations.

GAP is an independent group and its reports represent the composite findings and opinions of its members only, guided by its many consultants.

Toward Therapeutic Care (second edition) was formulated by the *Committee on Therapeutic Care*. The members of this committee as well as all other committees are listed below.

Committee on Therapeutic Care
Bernard H. Hall, Topeka, Chr.
Ian L. W. Clancey, Ottawa
Thomas E. Curtis, Chapel Hill
Robert W. Gibson, Towson, Md.
Harold A. Greenberg, Bethesda
Henry U. Grunebaum, Boston
Melvin Sabshin, Chicago
Benjamin Simon, Boston
Robert E. Switzer, Topeka

Committee on Adolescence
Joseph D. Noshpitz, Washington, Chr.
Warren J. Gadpaille, Denver
Mary O'Neil Hawkins, New York
Charles A. Malone, Philadelphia
Silvio J. Onesti, Jr., Boston
Vivian Rakoff, Toronto
Jeanne Spurlock, Nashville
Sidney L. Werkman, Denver

Committee on Aging
Jack Weinberg, Chicago, Chr.
Robert N. Butler, Washington, D.C.
Lawrence F. Greenleigh, Los Angeles
Maurice E. Linden, Philadelphia
Prescott W. Thompson, San Jose, Calif.
Montague Ullman, Brooklyn

Committee on Child Psychiatry
E. James Anthony, St. Louis, Chr.
James M. Bell, Canaan, N. Y.
H. Donald Dunton, New York
Joseph M. Green, Madison, Wis.
John F. Kenward, Chicago
William S. Langford, New York
John F. McDermott, Jr., Honolulu
Suzanne T. van Amerongen, Boston
Exie E. Welsch, New York
Virginia N. Wilking, New York

121

Committee on College Student
Robert L. Arnstein, New Haven, Chr.
Harrison P. Eddy, New York
Alfred Flarsheim, Chicago
Alan Frank, Albuquerque, N. M.
Malkah Tolpin Notman, Brookline, Mass.
Kent E. Robinson, Towson, Md.
Earle Silber, Chevy Chase, Md.
Tom G. Stauffer, Scarsdale, N. Y.

Committee on the Family
Norman L. Paul, Cambridge, Chr.
Ivan Boszormenyi-Nagy, Philadelphia
L. Murray Bowen, Chevy Chase
David Mendell, Houston
Joseph Satten, Topeka
Kurt O. Schlesinger, San Francisco
John P. Spiegel, Waltham, Mass.
Lyman C. Wynne, Bethesda
Israel Zwerling, New York

Committee on Governmental Agencies
Harold Rosen, Baltimore, Chr.
Calvin S. Drayer, Philadelphia
Edward O. Harper, Cleveland
John E. Nardini, Washington, D.C.
Donald B. Peterson, Fulton, Mo.

Committee on International Relations
Bryant M. Wedge, West Medford, Mass., Chr.
Francis F. Barnes, Chevy Chase
Eugene B. Brody, Baltimore
William D. Davidson, Washington, D.C.
Joseph T. English, Washington, D.C.
Louis C. English, Pomona, N. Y.
Frank Fremont-Smith, Massapequa, N. Y.
Robert L. Leopold, Philadelphia
John A. P. Millet, New York
Alain J. Sanseigne, New York
Bertram Schaffner, New York
Mottram P. Torre, New Orleans
Ronald Wintrob, Hartford

Committee on Medical Education
David R. Hawkins, Charlottesville, Chr.
Hugh T. Carmichael, Washington, D.C.
Robert S. Daniels, Chicago
Raymond Feldman, Boulder, Colo.
Saul I. Harrison, Ann Arbor

Harold I. Leif, Philadelphia
John E. Mack, Boston
William L. Peltz, Philadelphia
David S. Sanders, Los Angeles
Robert A. Senescu, Albuquerque, N. M.
Roy M. Whitman, Cincinnati

Committee on Mental Health Services
Lee G. Sewall, N. Little Rock, Ark., Chr.
Eugene M. Caffey, Jr., Washington
Morris E. Chafetz, Boston
Merrill Eaton, Omaha
James B. Funkhouser, Richmond, Va.
Robert S. Garber, Belle Mead, N. J.
Alan I. Levenson, Tucson, Ariz.
W. Walter Menninger, Topeka
Jack A. Wolford, Pittsburgh

Committee on Mental Retardation
Henry H. Work, Los Angeles, Chr.
Howard V. Bair, Parsons, Kans.
Peter W. Bowman, Pownal, Me.
Stuart M. Finch, Ann Arbor
Leo Madow, Philadelphia
Irving Philips, San Francisco
George Tarjan, Los Angeles
Warren T. Vaughan, Jr., San Mateo
Thomas G. Webster, Chevy Chase

Committee on Preventive Psychiatry
Stephen Fleck, New Haven, Chr.
Gerald Caplan, Boston
Jules V. Coleman, New Haven
Albert J. Glass, Oklahoma City
Benjamin Jeffries, Harper Woods, Mich.
E. James Lieberman, Washington, D.C.
Mary E. Mercer, Nyack, N. Y.
Harris B. Peck, Bronx, N. Y.
Marvin E. Perkins, New York
Harold M. Visotsky, Chicago

Committee on Psychiatry and Law
Alan A. Stone, Cambridge, Chr.
Edward T. Auer, St. Louis
John Donnelly, Hartford
Jay Katz, New Haven
Zigmond M. Lebensohn, Washington
Carl P. Malmquist, Minneapolis
Seymour Pollack, Los Angeles
Gene L. Usdin, New Orleans
Andrew S. Watson, Ann Arbor

122

124

ACKNOWLEDGMENTS

The program of the Group for the Advancement of Psychiatry, a non-profit, tax-exempt organization, is made possible largely through the voluntary contributions and efforts of its members. For their financial assistance during the past fiscal year, in helping it to fulfill its aims, GAP is grateful to the following foundations and organizations:

Sponsors

> THE COMMONWEALTH FUND
> THE DIVISION FUND
> MAURICE FALK MEDICAL FUND
> THE GRANT FOUNDATION
> THE GROVE FOUNDATION
> THE HOLZHEIMER FUND
> ITTLESON FAMILY FOUNDATION
> THE OLIN FOUNDATION
> OPPENHEIMER & CO. FOUNDATION, INC.
> A. H. ROBINS COMPANY
> ROCHE LABORATORIES
> SANDOZ PHARMACEUTICALS
> THE MURRAY L. SILBERSTEIN FUND
> SQUIBB INSTITUTE FOR MEDICAL RESEARCH
> SMITH KLINE & FRENCH FOUNDATION
> THE UPJOHN COMPANY
> WALLACE PHARMACEUTICALS
> WYETH LABORATORIES

Donors

> VIRGINIA & NATHAN BEDERMAN FOUNDATION
> GRALNICK FOUNDATION
> THE FOREST HOSPITAL FOUNDATION

125

PUBLICATIONS OF THE
GROUP FOR THE ADVANCEMENT OF PSYCHIATRY

Because readers of this publication may not be aware of other GAP titles on related subjects, a selected listing is given below.

Number	Title	Price
22	The Psychiatric Nurse in the Mental Hospital—May 1952	$ .10
46	Administration of the Public Psychiatric Hospital—July 1960	1.00
49	Reports in Psychotherapy: Initial Interviews—June 1961	.75
55	Public Relations: A Responsibility of the Mental Hospital Administrator—April 1963	.75
59	Psychiatry and the Aged: An Introductory Approach —Sept. 1965	1.00
61	Laws Governing Hospitalization of the Mentally Ill —May 1966	.50
70	The Nonpsychotic Alcoholic Patient and the Mental Hospital (A Position Statement)—Oct. 1968	.25
72	Crisis in Psychiatric Hospitalization—March 1969	1.00

Orders amounting to less than $3.00 must be accompanied by remittance. All prices are subject to change without notice.

GAP publications may be ordered on a subscription basis. The current subscription cycle comprising the Volume 7 Series covers the period from July 1, 1968 to June 30, 1971. The subscription fee is $12.00 U.S.A. and $13.00 Canadian and other foreign, payable in U.S. currency.

Bound volumes of GAP publications issued since 1947 are also available. They include GAP titles no longer in print that are unavailable in any other form.

Please send your order and remittance to: Publications Office, Group for the Advancement of Psychiatry, 419 Park Avenue South, New York, New York 10016.

This publication was produced for the Group for the Advancement of Psychiatry by the Mental Health Materials Center, Inc., New York.